2024
BABY GIRL
NAMES

_____

_____

Practical Tips and Advice for Choosing The Perfect Baby Girl Name

1. Personal Preference: Think about names that appeal to you and your partner.

2. Cultural Significance: If you want to honor a specific culture or ethnicity through your child's name, you might want to consider names that are traditional in that culture or have a special meaning.

3. Pronunciation and Spelling: Select a name that is simple to spell and pronounce. It can be aggravating for your child to have to correct people who mispronounce or misspell their name all the time.

4. Future Implications: Think about the long-term implications of the name you choose for your child. Will the name be appropriate for your child's entire life, including adulthood? Will the name be simple to say and spell in the professional world?

5.Top Trending: Think about names that are currently popular, such as Emma, Olivia, or Ava. Keep in mind, however, that popular names can become overused and lose their uniqueness over time.

6. Classic Names: Consider names that have been popular for generations, such as Elizabeth, Catherine, or Margaret.

7. Old Fashioned: Get ideas from names that were popular in the past, such as Mildred, Gertrude, or Ethel. These names could be making a comeback!

8. Unique & Uncommon Names: If you want to be truly unique, consider names that are less common, such as Azalea, Calliope, or Xanthe.

9. Vintage Names: Look into names that were popular in the past but have since become obsolete, such as Edith, Beatrice, or Agatha.

10. Badass Princess Names: Athena, Xena, and Zelda are examples of names that are both strong and feminine.

11. Strong Names: Names that convey strength and resilience, such as Brianna, Valentina, or Seraphina.

12. Virtue Names: Get ideas from names that embody positive virtues such as Hope, Faith, or Grace.

13. Literary Names: Look for names that are both unique and meaningful, such as Hermione, Scout, or Katniss, in your favorite books.

14. Mythology Names: Look into mythological names like Athena, Freya, or Persephone.

15. Nature Names: Names inspired by nature, such as Autumn, Willow, or Aurora.

Consider names inspired by colors, such as Scarlett, Violet, or Jade.

17. Place Names: Look for names inspired by locations such as Brooklyn, Paris, or Sydney.

18. Nicknames: Consider names that can be easily shortened into nicknames, such as Samantha (Sam), Alexandra (Alex), or Elizabeth (Lizzie).

19. Middle Names: Select a middle name that complements the first name and is in keeping with family traditions.

20. Unisex Names: Think about names that are appropriate for both boys and girls, such as Jordan, Charlie, or Riley.

21. International Names: Look into names from different cultures and languages, such as Amara, Niamh, or Svetlana.

22. Twin Names: Look for names that go well together, such as Olivia and Sophia, Ava and Mia, or Emma and Ella.

Table of content:

important:

Some names may appear in multiple categories because they have multiple meanings or associations. For example, the name Aurora may appear in both the Nature Names and Mythology Names categories because it is associated with both the natural phenomenon of the aurora borealis and the Roman goddess of dawn. Similarly, the name Scarlett may appear in both the Color Names and Literary Names categories because of its association with the color red and the protagonist of the novel "Gone with the Wind."

TOP
TRENDING NAMES

1. Abigail

This name is of Hebrew origin and means "cause of joy" or "father's joy". It was a common name in the Bible and is associated with happiness and positivity.

2. Addison

An Old English name meaning "son of Adam". It also translates to "Earth" from Hebrew origin.

3. Adeline

This name has French and German origins. It's a diminutive of Adele and means "noble" or "nobility".

4. Alice

Alice is of Old German origin and means "noble" or "nobility". It's a variant of the Old French name Adeliz, from Adelaide.

5. Amelia

Amelia is of Latin and Old German origin. It means "work" and is related to the name Amalia.

6. Anna

Anna is the Latin form of Hannah, a Hebrew name that is derived from the root chanan, meaning "grace".

7. Aria

Aria has Greek, Latin, Hebrew, and Persian roots. In Italian, Aria translates to "air" but also means song or melody.

8. Ariana

Ariana is a Latin name that was created from the Grecian name Ariani. This Grecian name came from the Persian word which was Ariyanem and meant "the land of the Persians".

9. Athena

Athena is a feminine name of Greek origin that comes from the Greek goddess Athena, who personifies wisdom, warfare, and craftwork.

10. Aubrey

Aubrey, of French and English origin, means "elf ruler". Originally a boys' name, Aubrey tipped the scales in 1974 and is now used 98% of the time for girls

11. Audrey

This name is of English origin and means "noble strength". It was originally a medieval diminutive of the name Etheldreda.

12. Aurora

This name is of Latin origin and it means "dawn". Aurora was the Roman goddess of the dawn.

13. Autumn

This name is of English origin and it comes from the Latin word "autumnus", which was first meant to describe the season that is more commonly known as the fall.

14. Ava

This name has multiple origins. It could be a variant of Eve or Eva, meaning "life" in Hebrew. It could also be of Latin origin, meaning "bird" or "birdlike".

15. Avery

This name is of English and French origin and it means "ruler of elves".

16. Ayla

This name is of Hebrew origin and it means "Oak Tree". It also has Turkish roots, which means "halo of light around the moon".

17. Bella

This name is of Italian and Latin origin and it means "beautiful". It can also be a short form of Isabella or Isabelle, which means "God's promise".

18. Brooklyn

This name is of American origin and it means "Broken Land Or Pretty Brook". It comes from the Dutch town named Breukelen, in Utrecht, The Netherlands.

19. Camila

This name is of Latin origin and it means "helper to the priest".

20. Caroline

This name is of French origin and it means "free man". It is the feminine version of Charles.

21. Charlotte

This name is of French origin and means "free man". It is the feminine form of Charles.

22. Chloe

Chloe Of Greek origin, Chloe means "green shoot", referring to new plant growth in the spring.

23. Claire

This name comes from a French word meaning "clear", "bright", or "light-colored".

24. Cora

Cora Of Greek origin, Cora means "maiden". It is probably a variant of Kore or Corinna.

25. Delilah

This name is of Hebrew origin and means "delicate" or "weak".

26. Eleanor

An English variation of the Provençal name Alienor, Eleanor means "light-hearted" or "shining light".

27. Elena

This name is of Greek, Italian, and Spanish origin and means "shining light".

28. Eliana

Of Hebrew and Greek origin, Eliana means "God has answered".

29. Elizabeth

Elizabeth This name is of Hebrew origin and means "God is my oath".

30. Ella

Ella Of Hebrew origin, Ella means "goddess" and is also associated with a tree in the pistachio family.

31. Ellie

Ellie This short and sweet name means "light" and has English and French origins. It first became popular in the United Kingdom as a nickname for Ellen or Eleanor.

32. Eloise

This name is of Old German origin, and the meaning of Eloise is "famous warrior". It is also associated with the Greek word Ἥλιος (helios) meaning "sun".

33. Emery

This name is of Old German origin, and the meaning of Emery is "brave," "powerful" or "ruler." It comes from the Old German name Emmerich, which can mean "labour ruler"

34. Emilia

This is a girl's name of Spanish and Italian origin, meaning "rival". Emilia is derived from the Latin name Aemilia.

35. Emily

This name is derived from the Roman family name Aemilius. The Aemilius family was prominent and powerful in ancient Rome. The name may come from the Latin word aemulus meaning "rival," or the Greek term aimylos meaning "wily" or "persuasive".

36. Emma

This name is of German origin meaning "whole" and "universal." Emma began as a shortened version of other Germanic names including Emily and even Ermintrude.

37. Evelyn

This name is of English and German origin. Possibly derived from the German name Eberhard, it combines the Old High German word eber, meaning "boar," with the English word "leigh," meaning "meadow".

38. Everleigh

This is a girl's name meaning "from the boar meadow" and is of English origin. The name Everleigh is derived from Old English and Saxon roots.

39. Everly

This name originated as a toponymic surname derived from the Old English roots eofor, meaning "boar," and leah, "clearing".

40. Evie

This name is of Hebrew origin meaning "life". Evie was derived from Eve, which in turn comes from Chawwah, a Hebrew name related to the concept of life.

41. Florence

This is an androgynous French and English given name. It is derived from the French version of (Saint) Florentia, a Roman martyr under Diocletian.

42. Freya

From Old Norse Freyja meaning "lady". This is the name of a goddess with love, beauty, war, and death in Norse mythology.

43. Gabriella

This is primarily a female name of Latin origin that means "God is my strength". It is the feminine form of Gabriel.

44. Genesis

This name is of English origin and means "origin" or "birth". It is also the name of the first book of the Bible.

45. Gianna

This is a girl's name of Italian origin meaning "the Lord is gracious". It originated as a diminutive for Giovanna- a Latin feminization of John.

46. Grace

This name is of Latin origin and was first used as a reference to the phrase "God's grace". Grace's meanings include charm, goodness, and generosity.

47. Hailey

The name Hailey is a Scottish clan name of English origin and means "Hay's meadow". It is also of Norse origin, meaning "hero" and Irish origin, meaning "wise one".

48. Hannah

This is a girl's name of Hebrew origin meaning "grace".

49. Harper

This name is of English, Scottish, and Irish origin. It is derived from the word "harp," referring to the musical stringed instrument, and means "someone who plays the harp".

50. Hazel

This name is of English origin and refers to the hazel plant and the greenish-brown color hazel.

51. Iris

This name is of Greek origin. Iris was the goddess of the rainbow in Greek mythology, and the name means "rainbow".

52. Isabella

This name is of Hebrew, Spanish, and Italian origin and means "pledged to God". It is a Latinate form of Isabel, a variation of Elizabeth.

53. Isla

This name is of Spanish origin and means "island". It also has Scottish origins, referring to Islay, an island off the west coast of Scotland.

54. Ivy

This name is of English and Latin origin and means "vine". It's derived from the Old English word for the ivy plant "ifig".

55. Jade

This name is of English origin and means "green gemstone".

56. Josephine

This name is of Hebrew origin and means "Jehovah increases". It is the feminine form of Joseph.

57. Kennedy

This name is of Irish and Scottish origin and means "chief with helmet" or "misshapen head".

58. Kinsley

This name is of Old English origin and means "king's meadow".

59. Layla

This name has Arabic and Hebrew origins. The most common meaning for the name in Arabic is "night," or "dark

60. Leah

This name comes from the Hebrew word la'ah, which means weary. It is found in he Old Testament of the Bible, notably in the book of Genesis.

61. Leilani

This is a Hawaiian given name meaning "heavenly garland of flowers" or "royal child". The Hawaiian word lei refers to flowers and lani to the sky or heavens, with an association with royalty.

62. Liliana

This name is a variant of the name Lily, as it still means "lily flower". Alternative meanings for this name include "purity, beauty, and innocence".

63. Lily

Derived from the Latin word "lilium," Lily represents purity, beauty, and grace. It is often associated with the enchanting flower of the same name, renowned for its delicate petals and intoxicating fragrance.

64. Lucy

The name Lucy is of Latin origin, and it means "light". It is derived from the masculine Lucius.

65. Luna

The name Luna is of Italian origin meaning "moon". The name of the Roman goddess of the moon, Luna is derived straight from the Latin word for moon, luna.

66. Lydia

The name Lydia is of Greek origin meaning "woman from Lydia". Lydia is one of the first place names, after an area of Asia Minor whose inhabitants are credited with strong musical talent and great wealth.

67. Madelyn

Madelyn is a girl's name that derives from a Hebrew word meaning "high tower." It evolved to the Greek name Magdalene and then the English version Madelyn.

68. Madison

Madison is a surname of English origin that has become a popular given name in the United States. Madison, also spelled Maddison, is a variant of Mathieson, meaning son of Matthew.

69. Maisie

This name is of English and Greek origin, meaning "pearl". It is a nickname for Margaret or Marjorie and was originally a Scottish variant of Margaret.

70. Margot

This name is of French origin, meaning "pearl". Margot originated as a French pet form of Marguerite, a name that ultimately derived from the Greek margarites.

71. Maria

This name is of Aramaic Latin origin, meaning "drop of the sea" or "bitter". The name is derived from the Hebrew name Miriam and the Egyptian name Mry, meaning "beloved".

72. Maya

This name has multiple origins and meanings. In Sanskrit, Maya means "dream" or "illusion". In Greek, Maya means "good mother". In Hebrew, it's a variation of the name Mayim, meaning "water".

73. Mia

This name is of Latin origin and means "mine". It is also a short form of Maria.

74. Mila

This name has multiple origins and meanings. In Spanish, Mila is derived from the name Milagros, which means "miracles." In Russian, it means "gracious" or "dear one".

75. Naomi

This name is of Hebrew origin, meaning "pleasantness".

76. Natalia

This name is of Latin origin, meaning 'relating to Christmas' or 'born on Christmas Day.' It comes from the Latin word 'natalis,' which means 'of or concerning birth'.

77. Natalie

This name is of French origin, meaning "birthday of the Lord". It is derived from the Latin phrase natale domini.

78. Nevaeh

This name is of American origin, meaning 'heaven.' This modern name is truly unique in its origin and was created by spelling heaven backward.

79. Nora

This name has several meanings. In Ireland, Nora is derived from the name Honora, which is in turn derived from the Latin word for honor. In France, the name Nora comes from the name Eleanora, which means "light."

80. Nova

This name is from the Latin word novus, which means new. It is also the name given to a star that beams with sudden and increasing brightness after exploding with a burst of energy.

81. Olivia

This name is of English origin and comes from the Latin word "oliva" meaning "olive." In ancient Rome, the olive tree was a symbol of peace and friendship.

82. Paisley

This name comes from the name of a town in Scotland, located close to Glasgow. People from the town of Paisley used it as their surname. which means church.

83. Penelope

This name is of Greek origin meaning "weaver". Penelope is a name from Greek mythology; she was the wife of Odysseus in Homer's Odyssey.

84. Quinn

This name is of Irish origin and means "descendant of Conn".

85. Raelynn

This is a modern, invented name, formed by a combination of the name Rae and the suffix 'lyn.' It can also be a combination of two names, Rae and Lynn meaning 'ewe,'.

86. Riley

This name has divergent meanings – "woods clearing" or "courageous/valiant" In the English tradition.

87. Ruby

This name is of Latin and French origin and means "deep red precious stone." It derives from the Latin word ruber, meaning red.

88. Sadie

This name is of Hebrew origin and means "princess". Sadie began as a nickname for Sarah.

89. Sarah

Sarah A name of Hebrew and Persian origin, often translated as "princess" or "woman of high rank". It's also interpreted as "noblewoman", "lady", or "happy". The first known Sarah was a major character in the Old Testament.

90. Savannah

Derived from the English word for the large grassy plain, ultimately deriving from the Taino (Native American) word zabana.

91. Scarlett

Scarlett An English name that comes from a surname for people who sold a luxurious wool cloth known as scarlet.

92. Serenity

Serenity A modern English name taken from the word "serenity" meaning "peaceful"

93. Sofia

A variant of the Greek name Sophia, derived directly from Sophia, the Greek word for wisdom.

94. Sophia

Sophia A name of Greek origin, derived from the word "sophos," meaning "wisdom". In ancient Greece, Sophia was the personification of wisdom and was often depicted as a goddess.

95. Stella

Derived from the Latin word "stella", meaning "star".

96. Valentina

Valentina A feminine form of the Roman name Valentinus, derived from the Latin word "valens" meaning "healthy, strong".

97. Victoria

A Latin name meaning "victory". It is the feminine variant of the masculine name, Victor.

98. Violet

Derived from the Latin word "viola", meaning "purple". It represents both the color purple and the flower of the same name.

99. Willow

A name of English origin, derived from the willow tree noted for its slender and graceful branches.

100. Zoey

A variant of Zoe, a name of Greek origin meaning "life".

Classic Names

1. Abbey: is derived from the Hebrew name Abigail and is a gender-neutral name that means "father of exalta⊠on."

2. Ada: a Germanic name that means "noble". It is also a Hebrew name that means "adornment".

3. Adeline: a French name that means "noble". It is a spelling variation of the name Adelaide.

4. Alexandra: is a Greek name that means "people's defender." It is a female version of the name Alexander.

5. Alice: a Germanic name that means "noble". It's also the name of the main character in Lewis Carroll's novel "Alice's Adventures in Wonderland."

6. Amelia: is a Germanic name meaning "work". It is also the name of Amelia Earhart, the first female aviator to fly solo across the Atlantic.

7. Amy is a French name that means "beloved." It is also a spelling variation of the name Amata.

8. Anna is a Hebrew name that means "grace". Anna was the mother of the Virgin Mary in the Bible.

9. Anne is a French name that means "grace". It is also a spelling variation of the name Anna.

10. Audrey: is an English name meaning "noble strength". Audrey Hepburn is also known by this name.

11. Ava: is a Latin name meaning "life". It is also a spelling variation of the name Eve.

12. Beatrice: is a Latin name meaning "she who brings happiness". It is also a character name in Dante's "Divine Comedy."

13. Caroline: is a French name meaning "free man". It is a female version of the name Charles.

14. Catherine: is a Greek name meaning "pure". It's also the name of several saints and queens.

15. Cecilia: a Latin name that means "blind". It is also the name of music's patron saint.

16. Charlotte: a French name that means "free man" Several queens and princesses have been given this name.

17. Chloe: a Greek name that means "blooming". It is also the name of a New Testament character.

18. Claire: is a French name meaning "clear".

18. Claire: is a French name meaning "clear". It is also the name of several saints.

19. Clara: is a Latin name meaning "bright". Clara Barton, the founder of the Red Cross, was also given this name.

20. Cora: is a Greek name meaning "maiden". It's also a character name in James Fenimore Cooper's "The Last of the Mohicans."

21. Daisy: is an English name meaning "day's eye". It's also the name of a type of flower.

22. Diana: is a Latin name meaning "divine". Diana is the goddess of the hunt and the moon in Roman mythology.

23. Dorothy: is a Greek name that means "gift of God." It is also the protagonist's name in L. Frank Baum's "The Wizard of Oz."

24. Edith: is an English name meaning "prosperous in war". It is also the name of several saints.

25. Eleanor: is a French name that means "bright, shining one." It's also the name of a few queens.

26. Elizabeth: is a Hebrew name that means "God is my oath." It's also the name of several queens and saints.

27. Emily is a Latin name that means "rival". It is also the name of the main character in Charlotte Bronte's novel "Wuthering Heights."

28. Emma: is a Germanic name that means "universal". It's also the name of the main character in Jane Austen's "Emma."

29. Esther: a Hebrew name that means "star" Esther was a Persia queen who saved the Jewish people from genocide in the Bible.

30. Evelyn: is a French name that means "hazelnut". It is also the name of several saints.

31. Flora: is a Latin name that means "flower". Flora is the goddess of flowers and spring in Roman mythology.

32. Florence: is a Latin name that means "thriving." It is also the name of several saints.

33. Gabrielle: is a French name that means "God is my strength." It is a female version of the name Gabriel.

34. Genevieve: is a French name that means "woman of the people." It is also the name of Paris' patron saint.

35. Georgia: is a Greek name that means "farmer." In addition, it is the name of a state in the United States.

36. Grace: is an English name that means "God's grace." It is also a name of virtue.

37. Gwendoline: a Welsh name that means "white ring" It is also a spelling variation of the name Gwendolyn.

38. Hannah: is a Hebrew name that means "grace". Hannah was the mother of the prophet Samuel in the Bible.

39. Harriet: is an English name that means "ruler of the home." Harriet Tubman, an abolitionist, was also given this name.

40. Hazel: a name that means "hazel tree" in English. It also serves as the name of a color.

41. Helen: is a Greek name that means "bright, shining one." Helen was the daughter of Zeus and Leda in Greek mythology, and she was known as the most beautiful woman in the world.

42. Imogen: Imogen is a Celtic name that means "maiden". It is also a character name in Shakespeare's play "Cymbeline."

43. Isabella: is a Hebrew name that means "God is my oath." It is also a spelling variation of the name Elizabeth.

44. Isabelle: is a French name that means "God is my oath." It is also a spelling variation of the name Elizabeth.

45. Ivy: is a name that means "faithfulness" in English. It's also the name of a type of climbing plant.

46. Jane: is an English name that means "God is gracious." It is also the name of the main character in Charlotte Bronte's novel "Jane Eyre."

47. Josephine: is a French name that means "God will increase". It is also the name of Napoleon Bonaparte's wife.

48. Julia: is a Latin name that means "youthful". It's also the name of a couple of saints and empresses.

49. Juliette: is a French name that means "youthful". It's also the name of the main character in Shakespeare's "Romeo and Juliet."

50. Kate: is an English name that means "pure". It is also a short form of the name Katherine.

51. Katherine: is a Greek name that means "pure". It's also the name of several

saints and queens.

52. Laura: is a Latin name that means "laurel". It is also the name of several saints.

53. Lillian: is an English name that means "lily". It is also a spelling variation of the name Lily.

54. Lily: is an English name that means "lily flower." It's also the name of a type of flower.

55. Louisa: is a French name that means "renowned warrior." Louisa May Alcott was also given this name.

56. Lucy: a Latin name that means "light" It is also a saint's name.

57. Lydia: is a Greek name that means "from Lydia". Lydia was a purple cloth seller who was converted to Christianity by the apostle Paul in the Bible.

58. Mabel: is an English name that means "lovable." It was a popular name in the late 1800s and early 1900s.

59. Madeline: is a French name that means "woman from Magdala." Mary Magdalene was a disciple of Jesus in the Bible.

60. Margaret: is a Greek name that means "pearl". It's also the name of several saints and queens.

61. Maria: is a Latin name that means "bitter". It is also the name of Jesus' mother.

62. Martha: an Aramaic name that means "lady" Martha was the sister of Mary and Lazarus in the Bible.

63. Mary is a Hebrew name that means "bitter". It is also the name of Jesus' mother.

64. Matilda: a Germanic name that means "mighty in battle." It is also the name of England's queen.

65. Naomi: is a Hebrew name that means "pleasantness." Naomi was Ruth's mother-in-law in the Bible.

66. Natalie: is a French name that means "born on Christmas day." It is also a spelling variation of the name Natalia.

67. Nora: is an Irish name that means "honor". It is also a short form of the name Honora.

68. Olive: means "olive tree" in English. It is also a peace symbol.

69. Olivia: a Latin name that means "olive tree" It is also a character name in Shakespeare's play "Twelfth Night."

70. Pearl: is a name that means "pearl" in English. It also represents purity.

71. Penelope: a Greek name that means "weaver". Penelope was Odysseus' wife in Greek mythology.

72. Phoebe: is a Greek name that means "bright, shining one." Phoebe was a deaconess in the early Christian church in the Bible.

73. . Rachel: is a Hebrew name that means "ewe". Rachel was Jacob's wife and the mother of Joseph and Benjamin in the Bible.

74. Rebecca: is a Hebrew name that means "to tie, to bind." Rebecca was Isaac's wife and the mother of Jacob and Esau in the Bible.

75. Rose: an English name that means "rose flower" It's also the name of a type of flower.

74. Ruby: is a name that means "red gemstone" in English. It is also a love symbol.

76. Ruth: is a Hebrew name that means "friendship". Ruth was a Moabite woman who became King David's great-grandmother in the Bible.

77. Sarah: a Hebrew name that means "princess" Sarah was Abraham's wife and Isaac's mother in the Bible.

78. Sophia: is a Greek name that means "wisdom" in English. It is also the name of several saints.

79. Stella: is a Latin name that means "star". It's also a character name in Tennessee Williams' play "A Streetcar Named Desire."

80. Victoria: a Latin name that means "victory" It is also the name of the Roman victory goddess.

81. Violet: is a name that means "purple flower" in English. It's also the name of a type of flower.

82. Vivian: is a Latin name that means "lively". It is also the name of several saints.

Old Fashionned Names

1. Adah: is a Hebrew name meaning "ornament" or "adornment". It is a biblical name and a classic choice for a baby girl.

2. Adelaide: is a German name meaning "noble kind" or "of noble birth". It is a vintage name that has been gaining popularity in recent years.

3. Adeline: is a French name meaning "noble" or "nobility". It is a classic and elegant name.

4. Agatha: is a Greek name meaning "good" or "kind". It is an old-fashioned name that has been making a comeback in recent years.

5. Agnes: is a Greek name meaning "pure" or "chaste". It is a classic and timeless name.

6. Alexandra: is a Greek name meaning "defender of the people". It is a strong and regal name.

7. Alice: is a German name meaning "noble" or "of noble birth". It is a classic and timeless name.

8. Alma: is a Latin name meaning "nurturing" or "kind". It is a simple and sweet name.

9. Alva: is a Scandinavian name meaning "elf" or "magical being". It is a unique and mystical name.

10. Amabel: is a Latin name meaning "lovable" or "worthy of love". It is a charming and vintage name.

11. Annabelle: is a combination of the names Anna and Belle, meaning "graceful" and "beautiful". It is a sweet and feminine name.

12. Aphra: is a Hebrew name meaning "dust" or "ashes". It is a unique and uncommon name.

13. Beatrice: is a Latin name meaning "bringer of joy" or "blessed". It is a classic and elegant name.

14. Beatrix: is a Latin name meaning "voyager" or "blessed". It is a unique and strong name.

15. Belinda: is a German name meaning "bright serpent" or "beautiful snake". It is a unique and mystical name.

16. Beverly: is an English name meaning "beaver stream". It is a vintage and charming name.

17. Birdie: is an English name meaning "little bird". It is a cute and playful name.

18. Camelia: is a Latin name meaning "helper to the priest". It is a unique and elegant name.

19. Cecilia: is a Latin name meaning "blind" or "dim-sighted". It is a classic and timeless name.

20. Celeste: is a Latin name meaning "heavenly" or "of the sky". It is a beautiful and elegant name.

21. Clara: is a Latin name meaning "bright" or "clear". It is a classic and timeless name.

22. Clementine: is a French name meaning "merciful" or "gentle". It is a vintage and charming name.

23. Cleo: is a Greek name meaning "glory" or "fame". It is a short and strong name.

24. Cordelia: is a Latin name meaning "heart" or "daughter of the sea". It is a unique and elegant name.

25. Daphne: is a Greek name meaning "laurel tree" or "bay tree". It is a nature-inspired and unique name.

26. Delilah: is a Hebrew name meaning "delicate" or "weakened". It is a unique and mystical name.

27. Della: is a German name meaning "noble" or "of noble birth". It is a vintage and charming name.

28. Doris: is a Greek name meaning "gift" or "ocean". It is a classic and timeless name.

29. Edna: is a Hebrew name meaning "pleasure" or "delight". It is a vintage and charming name.

30. Effie: is a Greek name meaning "well-spoken" or "pleasant speech". It is a cute and playful name.

31. Elsie: is a Scottish name meaning "pledged to God". It is a diminutive of the name Elizabeth and has a vintage charm.

32. Enid: is a Welsh name meaning "soul" or "life". It is a unique and uncommon name.

33. Eudora: is a Greek name meaning "good gift". It is a rare and elegant name.

34. Eunice: is a Greek name meaning "good victory". It is a classic and timeless name.

35. Faye: is a French name meaning "fairy". It is a whimsical and enchanting name.

36. Fern: is an English name meaning "fern plant". It is a nature-inspired name that has been gaining popularity in recent years.

37. Flora: is a Latin name meaning "flower". It is a classic and elegant name.

38. Gilda: is a German name meaning "golden". It is a vintage name that has been making a comeback in recent years.

39. Greta: is a German name meaning "pearl". It is a simple and sweet name.

40. Harriet: is an English name meaning "ruler of the home". It is a classic and timeless name.

41. Hattie: is a diminutive of the name Harriet, meaning "ruler of the home". It is a vintage name that has been gaining popularity in recent years.

42. Hazel: is an English name meaning "hazel tree". It is a nature-inspired name that has been gaining popularity in recent years.

43. Henrietta: is a French name meaning "ruler of the home". It is a classic and elegant name.

44. Hester: is a Greek name meaning "star". It is a unique and uncommon name.

45. Hortense: is a French name meaning "gardener". It is a vintage name that has been making a comeback in recent years.

46. Ingrid: is a Scandinavian name meaning "beautiful". It is a strong and regal name.

47. Iola: is a Greek name meaning "violet-colored dawn". It is a unique and uncommon name.

48. Irene: is a Greek name meaning "peace". It is a classic and timeless name.

49. Iris: is a Greek name meaning "rainbow". It is a nature-inspired name that has been gaining popularity in recent years.

50. Isadora: is a Greek name meaning "gift of Isis". It is a unique and elegant name.

51. Ivy: is an English name meaning "ivy plant". It is a nature-inspired name that has been gaining popularity in recent years.

52. Josephine: is a French name meaning "God will add". It is a classic and elegant name.

53. Judith: is a Hebrew name meaning "woman of Judea". It is a classic and timeless name.

54. Juniper: is a Latin name meaning "youth-producing". It is a nature-inspired name that has been gaining popularity in recent years.

55. Lavinia: is a Latin name meaning "purity". It is a classic and elegant name.

56. Leona: is a Latin name meaning "lioness". It is a strong and regal name.

57. Lillian: is an English name meaning "lily". It is a classic and timeless name.

58. Loretta: is a Latin name meaning "crowned with laurel". It is a vintage name that has been making a comeback in recent years.

59. Lorraine: is a French name meaning "from Lorraine". It is a vintage name that has been making a comeback in recent years.

60. Lucille: is a French name meaning "light". It is a classic and elegant name.

61. Mabel: is an English name meaning "lovable". It was popular in the late 19th and early 20th centuries and has a vintage charm.

62. Maeve: is an Irish name meaning "intoxicating". It is a strong and unique name.

63. Marcella: is a Latin name meaning "warlike". It is a classic and elegant name.

64. Marjorie: is a French name meaning "pearl". It was popular in the early 20th century and has a vintage charm.

65. Maxine: is a Latin name meaning "greatest". It is a strong and modern name.

66. Mildred: is an English name meaning "gentle strength". It was popular in the early 20th century and has a vintage charm.

67. Minerva: is a Latin name meaning "wisdom". It is the name of the Roman goddess of wisdom and has a strong and powerful connotation.

68. Myrtle: is a Greek name meaning "an aromatic shrub". It is a unique and uncommon name.

69. Nellie: is an English name meaning "bright, shining one". It is a diminutive of the name Eleanor and has a vintage charm.

70. Opal: is a Sanskrit name meaning "precious stone". It is a unique and uncommon name.

71. Ophelia: is a Greek name meaning "help". It is the name of a character in Shakespeare's play "Hamlet" and has a literary and romantic connotation.

72. Pauline: is a French name meaning "small". It is a diminutive of the name Paula and has a vintage charm.

73. Pearl: is an English name meaning "pearl". It is a classic and elegant name.

74. Priscilla: is a Latin name meaning "ancient". It is a classic and elegant name.

75. Ramona: is a Spanish name meaning "wise protector". It is a strong and modern name.

76. Regina: is a Latin name meaning "queen". It is a classic and elegant name.

77. Rosalind: is a Latin name meaning "pretty rose". It is a classic and elegant name.

78. Rosamund: is a German name meaning "horse protection". It is a unique and uncommon name.

79. Rosetta: is an Italian name meaning "little rose". It is a diminutive of the name Rose and has a romantic connotation.

80. Rowena: is a Welsh name meaning "white, fair". It is a unique and uncommon name.

81. Sabrina: is a Latin name meaning "from the river Severn". It is the name of a character in Shakespeare's play "The Tempest" and has a literary and romantic connotation.

82. Selma: is a German name meaning "divine helmet". It is a unique and uncommon name.

83. Sybil: is a Greek name meaning "prophetess". It is a classic and elegant name.

84. Thelma: is a Greek name meaning "will, volition". It was popular in the early 20th century and has a vintage charm.

85. Theodora: is a Greek name meaning "gift of God". It is a classic and elegant name.

86. Trudy: is a German name meaning "spear of strength". It is a diminutive of the name Gertrude and has a vintage charm.

87. Ursula: is a Latin name meaning "little bear". It is a classic and elegant name.

88. Veda: is a Sanskrit name meaning "knowledge". It is a unique and uncommon name.

89. Velma: is an English name meaning "will, desire". It was popular in the early 20th century and has a vintage charm.

90. Vera: is a Russian name meaning "faith". It is a classic and elegant name.

91. Verity: is a Latin name meaning "truth". It is a unique and uncommon name.

92. Viola: is a Latin name meaning "violet". It is a classic and elegant name.

93. Virginia: is a Latin name meaning "virgin". It is a classic and elegant name.

94. Vivienne: is a French name meaning "alive". It is a unique and uncommon name.

95. Winifred: is a Welsh name meaning "blessed peacemaking". It was popular in the early 20th century and has a vintage charm.

96. Wren: is an English name meaning "small bird". It is a unique and uncommon name.

97. Yvonne: is a French name meaning "yew tree". It is a classic and elegant name.

98. Zelda: is a Yiddish name meaning "blessed". It is a unique and uncommon name.

99. Zelma: is a German name meaning "helmet of God". It was popular in the early 20th century and has a vintage charm.

Unique & Uncommon Names

1. Adalee: is a mixture of Ada and Lee, which indicate "noble" and "meadow" respectively. It's a name synonymous with grace and beauty.

2. Adira: is a Hebrew name that means "strong" or "noble". It's a name that evokes strength and bravery.

3. Aella: is a Greek name that means "whirlwind" or "storm". It is a name linked with strength and force.

4. Agatha: a Greek name that means "good" or "kind". It is a name that embodies generosity and friendliness.

5. Alara: a Turkish name that means "red apple" It's a name that conjures up images of beauty and sweetness.

6. Althea is a Greek name that means "healer" or "wholesome". It is a name associated with health and well-being.

7. Alva: a Scandinavian name that means "elf" It's a name that conjures up images of enchantment and mystery.

8. Amara: is a Greek name that means "eternal" or "unfading". It is a name that denotes endurance and longevity.

9. Anais: is a French name that means "grace". It is a name linked with beauty and elegance.

10. Anika: a German name that means "grace" or "favor". It is a name that embodies generosity and friendliness.

11. Anouk: is a French name that means "grace". It is a name linked with beauty and elegance.

12. Aphra: is a Hebrew name that means "dust". It is a name that is associated with humility and simplicity.

13. Arden: is an English name that means "eagle valley." It's a name connected with independence and strength.

14. Aria: Aria is an Italian name that means "air" or "song". It's a name that embodies both innovation and beauty.

15. Artemis: a Greek name that means "goddess of the hunt." It's a name that connotes power and independence.

16. Astrid: is a Scandinavian name that means "divinely beautiful." It is a name associated with beauty and grace.

17. Azalea: a Greek name that means "dry". It's a name synonymous with beauty and elegance.

18. Belinda: a German name that means "bright serpent" or "beautiful". It is a name associated with beauty and grace.

19. Beverly: means "beaver stream" in English. It is a name linked with strength and resolve.

20. Briar: a word that means "thorny bush" in English. It is a name that embodies strength and resilience.

21. Calista: is a Greek name that means "most beautiful" or "most lovely." It is a name linked with beauty and grace.

22. Calla: is a Greek name that means "beautiful". It is a name that evokes beauty and elegance.

23. Camelia: is a Latin name that means "priest's assistant." It is a name linked with love and giving.

24. Celestia: a Latin name that means "heavenly" It is a name that evokes beauty and grace.

25. Cleo: is a Greek name that means "glory" or "fame". It's a name that connotes knowledge and wisdom.

26. Coralie: is a French name that means "coral". It is a name associated with beauty and elegance.

27. Cordelia: is a Celtic name that means "daughter of the sea." It's a name that connotes power and independence.

28. Cressida: is a Greek name that means "gold". It is a name associated with beauty and elegance.

29. Danica: a Slavic name that means "morning star" It is a name linked with light and direction.

30. Daphne: is a Greek name that means "laurel tree." It's a name that evokes strength and fortitude.

31. Delaney: is an Irish name that means "from the alder grove." It is a name connected with fortitude and perseverance.

32. Elara: is a Greek name that means "bright" or "shining". It's a name that embodies beauty and brilliance.

33. Electra: is a Greek name that means "amber" or "shining". It is a name linked with power and strength.

34. Elowen: a Cornish name that means "elm tree" It's a name that evokes strength

strength and fortitude.

35. Elysia: is a Greek name that means "joyful" or "heavenly." It is a name connected with joy and happiness.

36. Ember: an English name that means "spark" or "burning low". It is a name that evokes passion and fervor.

37. Esme: is a French name that means "beloved" or "esteemed." It's a name that conjures up feelings of love and affection.

38. Evangeline: is a Greek name that means "bearer of good news." It's a name that evokes optimism and hope.

39. Fable: is an English name that means "story" or "legend". It's a one-of-a-kind and uncommon name.

40. Fallon: an Irish name that means "leader" or "superior". It is a name linked with power and strength.

41..Freya: is a Scandinavian name that means "lady" or "mistress". It is a name associated with beauty and grace.

42. Gaia: is a Greek name that means "earth." It's a name linked to nature and the environment.

43. Galadriel: Galadriel is a fictional name from J.R.R. Tolkien's "The Lord of the Rings," which means "maiden crowned with a radiant garland." It's a name that embodies both beauty and strength.

44. Genevieve: is a French name that means "woman of the people." It is a name linked with generosity and benevolence.

45. Giselle: is a French name that means "pledge" or "oath." It is a name that emphasizes loyalty and dedication.

46. Guinevere: is a Welsh name that means "white shadow" or "white wave". It is a name linked with grace and beauty.

47. Harlow: an English name that means "rock hill" It's a name that evokes strength and fortitude.

48. Haven: is an English name that means "safe place" or "refuge". It is a name connected with security and protection.

49. Hera: is a Greek name that means "queen of the gods." It is a name associated with strength and force.

50. Imara: is a Swahili name that means "strong" or "firm". It is a name connected with fortitude and perseverance.

51. Inara: means "ray of light" in Arabic. It's a name that embodies beauty and

brilliance.

52. Indira: is a Sanskrit name that means "beauty" or "splendor". It is a name linked with grace and beauty.

53. Isabeau: is a French name that means "God is my oath." It is a name that emphasizes loyalty and dedication.

54. Isla: is a Scottish name that means "island." It's a name linked to nature and the environment.

55. Isolde: means "ice ruler" in German. It's a name that evokes strength and fortitude.

56. Jinx: is an English name that means "curse" or "spell". It's a one-of-a-kind and uncommon name.

57. Jocasta: is a Greek name that means "shining moon." It is a name connected with brilliance and beauty.

58. Juniper: is an English name that means "evergreen shrub." It's a name that evokes strength and fortitude.

59. Juno: is a Roman name that means "queen of the gods." It is a name linked with power and strength.

60. Kaia: is a Hawaiian name that means "sea". It is a name associated with nature and the environment.

61. Kallista: a Greek name that means "most beautiful." It is a name linked with grace and beauty.

62. Katarina: a Greek name that means "pure". It is a name associated with purity and innocence.

63. Kismet: is a Turkish name that means "fate" or "destiny." It's a one-of-a-kind and uncommon name.

64. Lark: an English name that means "songbird" It's a name linked to nature and the environment.

65. Lavinia: a Latin name that means "purity" It is a name associated with purity and innocence.

66. Lenora: a Greek name that means "light" It's a moniker synonymous with brilliance and beauty.

67. Lilith: is a Hebrew name that means "night monster" or "ghost". It's a name that conjures up images of mystery and gloom.

68. Liora: a Hebrew name that means "my light" It is a name associated with brilliance and beauty.

69. Lorelei: Lorelei is a German name that means "alluring enchantress". It's a name synonymous with beauty and charm.

70. Lyra: is a Greek name that means "lyre". It's a name linked to music and creativity.

71. Maelle: is a French name that means "chief" or "prince". It is a name linked with strength and leadership.

72. Magnolia: is a Latin name that means "flower of the magnolia." It's a name linked to nature and the environment.

73. Marcella: is a Latin name that means "warlike". It is a name linked with power and strength.

74. Maven: is a Yiddish name that means "expert" or "connoisseur". It's a one-of-a-kind and uncommon name.

75. Mira: is a Sanskrit name that means "wonderful" or "peace". It's a name synonymous with beauty and calm.

76. Morgana: is a Welsh name that means "sea circle." It is a name connected with enchantment and mystery.

77. Nixie: is a German name that means "water sprite." It's a name linked to nature and the environment.

78. Nola: is an Irish name that means "famous." It's a name synonymous with fame and fortune.

79. Oaklynn: a name that means "oak tree" in English. It's a name linked to nature and the environment.

80. Octavia: is a Latin name that means "eighth". It is a name linked with power and strength.

81. Odessa: is a Greek name that means "long journey." It's a name that conjures up images of adventure and travel.

82. Odette: is a French name that means "wealthy". It's a name synonymous with success and fortune.

83. Ophelia: is a Greek name that means "help". It is a name connected with compassion and charity.

84. Pandora: is a Greek name that means "all gifted." It's a name that connotes brilliance and creativity.

85. Persephone: is a Greek name that means "bringer of destruction." It is a name linked with power and strength.

86. Piper: is an English name that means "flute player." It's a name linked to music

and creativity.

87. Raina: is a Slavic name that means "queen". It is a name linked with power and strength.

88. Ravenna: is an Italian name that means "raven". It's a name that conjures up images of mystery and gloom.

89. Rhiannon: is a Welsh name that means "great queen." It is a name linked with power and strength.

90. Rosalind: a Latin name that means "pretty rose" It is a name linked with grace and beauty.

91. Rosalyn: is a spelling variation of Rosalind. It is also a Latin name that means "pretty rose".

92. Rowena: is a Welsh name that means "famous friend." It's a name that connotes friendship and commitment.

93. Sabine: is a Latin name that means "of the Sabine tribe." It is a name connected with fortitude and perseverance.

94. Sapphira: is a Greek name that means "sapphire". It's a name synonymous with beauty and elegance.

95. Selene: is a Greek name that means "moon goddess." It's a name that conjures up images of beauty and mystery.

96. Serafina: is a Latin name that means "fiery ones." It's a name that conjures up images of passion and ferocity.

97. Seraphina: is a feminine form of the name Serafina. It is also a Latin name that means "the fiery ones."

98. Seren: is a Welsh name that means "star". It is a name connected with brilliance and beauty.

99. Serenity: is a name that means "calmness" in English. It is a name linked with tranquillity and calm.

100. Talia: is a Hebrew name that means "dew from heaven." It is a name that connotes purity and freshness.

101. Talitha: is a Hebrew name that means "little girl." It's a name that conjures up images of childhood and innocence.

102. Thalia: is a Greek name that means "to blossom." It's a name synonymous with beauty and progress.

103. Theodora: is a Greek name that means "God's gift." It is a name linked with power and strength.

104. Thora: is a Scandinavian name that means "thunder". It is a name linked with power and strength.

105. Valencia: is a Spanish name that means "brave". It is a name that is connected with bravery and strength.

106. Valentina: is a Latin name that means "strong, healthy." It is a name linked with vigor and vigor.

107. Valkyrie: is a Norse name that means "chooser of the slain." It is a name linked with power and strength.

108. Veda: is a Sanskrit name that means "knowledge." It's a name that connotes wisdom and intelligence.

109. Vesper: a Latin name that means "evening star" It is a name connected with brilliance and beauty.

110. Vespera: is a spelling variation of the name Vesper. It's also a Latin name that means "evening star."

111. Vida: is a Spanish name that means "life". It is a name that evokes vitality and enthusiasm.

112. Wren: is an English name that means "small bird." It's a name linked to nature and the environment.

113. Xanthe: a Greek name that means "yellow". It is a name connected with light and brightness.

114. Xena: a Greek name that means "guest, stranger". It's a name that conjures up images of adventure and travel.

115. Xiomara: a Spanish name that means "prepared for battle." It is a name that connotes strength and power.

116. Yara is a Brazilian name that means "water lady." It is a name linked with the environment and nature.

117. Zahara: a Hebrew name that means "flowering". It is a beautiful and growing name.

118. Zara: is a Hebrew name that means "princess." It's a name that conjures up images of nobility and elegance.

119. Zenobia: is a Greek name that means "Life of Zeus." It is a name that connotes strength and power.

120. Zephyra: a Greek name that means "west wind." It is a name linked with the environment and nature.

121. Zinnia: is a Latin name that means "flower."

Vintage Names

1. Agatha: is a Greek name meaning "good" or "kind". It is a name associated with virtue and goodness.

2. Agnes: is a Greek name meaning "pure" or "chaste". It is a name associated with purity and innocence.

3. Alva: is a Scandinavian name meaning "elf" or "elfin". It is a name associated with magical and ethereal qualities.

4. Aphra: is a Hebrew name meaning "dust" or "ashes". It is a name associated with humility and mortality.

5. Belinda: is a Germanic name meaning "bright serpent" or "beautiful serpent". It is a name associated with beauty and grace.

6. Beverly: is an English name meaning "beaver stream". It is a name associated with nature and water.

7. Camelia: is a Latin name derived from the flower name Camellia. It is a name associated with beauty and elegance.

8. Cleo: is a Greek name meaning "glory" or "fame". It is a name associated with strength and success.

9. Cordelia: is a Celtic name meaning "heart" or "daughter of the sea". It is a name associated with love and femininity.

10. Daphne: is a Greek name meaning "laurel tree". It is a name associated with victory and honor.

11. Delilah: is a Hebrew name meaning "delicate" or "weak". It is a name associated with beauty and seduction.

12. Della: is a German name meaning "noble" or "of the nobility". It is a name associated with nobility and grace.

13. Doris: is a Greek name meaning "gift of the ocean". It is a name associated with the sea and water.

14. Edna: is a Hebrew name meaning "pleasure" or "delight". It is a name associated with joy and happiness.

15. Effie: is a Greek name meaning "well-spoken" or "eloquent". It is a name associated with intelligence and communication.

16. Elsie: is a Scottish name meaning "pledged to God". It is a name associated with devotion and faith.

17. Enid: is a Welsh name meaning "soul" or "life". It is a name associated with vitality and energy.

18. Eudora: is a Greek name meaning "good gift". It is a name associated with generosity and kindness.

19. Eunice: is a Greek name meaning "good victory". It is a name associated with triumph and success.

20. Faye: is an English name meaning "fairy" or "fairy-like". It is a name associated with enchantment and magic.

21. Fern: is an English name derived from the plant name. It is a name associated with nature and resilience.

22. Flora: is a Latin name meaning "flower". It is a name associated with beauty and nature.

23. Gilda: is a Germanic name meaning "golden". It is a name associated with brightness and radiance.

24. Greta: is a German name meaning "pearl". It is a name associated with purity and elegance.

25. Harriet: is an English name meaning "ruler of the home" or "estate ruler". It is a name associated with leadership and authority.

26. Hattie: is a diminutive of the name Harriet, meaning "ruler of the home" or "estate ruler". It is a name associated with strength and independence.

27. Hazel: is an English name derived from the hazel tree. It is a name associated with wisdom and protection.

28. Henrietta: is a French name meaning "ruler of the home" or "estate ruler". It is a name associated with leadership and power.

29. Hester: is a Greek name meaning "star". It is a name associated with brightness and guidance.

30. Hortense: is a Latin name meaning "gardener". It is a name associated with nature and nurturing.

31. Ingrid: is a Scandinavian name meaning "beautiful" or "fair". It is a name associated with beauty and grace.

32. Iola: is a Greek name meaning "violet-colored dawn". It is a name associated with new beginnings and freshness.

33. Irene: is a Greek name meaning "peace". It is a name associated with harmony and tranquility.

34. Iris: is a Greek name meaning "rainbow". It is a name associated with beauty

beauty and color.

35. Isadora: is a Greek name meaning "gift of Isis". It is a name associated with femininity and grace.

36. Ivy: is an English name derived from the ivy plant. It is a name associated with strength and resilience.

37. Josephine: is a French name meaning "God will add". It is a name associated with blessings and abundance.

38. Judith: is a Hebrew name meaning "woman of Judea". It is a name associated with strength and courage.

39. Juniper: is an English name derived from the juniper tree. It is a name associated with protection and healing.

40. Lavinia: is a Latin name meaning "purity". It is a name associated with innocence and virtue.

41. Leona: is a Latin name meaning "lioness". It is a name associated with strength and courage.

42. Lillian: is an English name derived from the flower name Lily. It is a name associated with purity and beauty.

43. Loretta: is a Latin name meaning "laurel". It is a name associated with honor and victory.

44. Lorraine: is a French name derived from the region of Lorraine in France. It is a name associated with tradition and heritage.

45. Lucille: is a French name meaning "light". It is a name associated with brightness and clarity.

46. Mabel: is an English name meaning "lovable". It is a name associated with affection and charm.

47. Maeve: is an Irish name meaning "intoxicating". It is a name associated with allure and enchantment.

48. Marcella: is a Latin name meaning "warlike". It is a name associated with strength and bravery.

49. Marjorie: is an English name derived from the herb marjoram. It is a name associated with warmth and comfort.

50. Maxine: is a Latin name meaning "greatest". It is a name associated with power and leadership.

51. Mildred: is an English name meaning "gentle strength". It is a name associated with resilience and kindness.

52. Minerva: is a Latin name derived from the Roman goddess of wisdom. It is a name associated with intelligence and wisdom.

53. Myrtle: is a Greek name derived from the myrtle tree. It is a name associated with love and fertility.

54. Nellie: is a diminutive of the name Helen, meaning "bright" or "shining light". It is a name associated with illumination and clarity.

55. Opal: is a gemstone name derived from the opal gem. It is a name associated with beauty and transformation.

56. Ophelia: is a Greek name meaning "help" or "aid". It is a name associated with compassion and support.

57. Pauline: is a feminine form of the name Paul, meaning "small" or "humble". It is a name associated with humility and modesty.

58. Pearl: is an English name derived from the gemstone pearl. It is a name associated with purity and elegance.

59. Priscilla: is a Latin name meaning "ancient" or "venerable". It is a name associated with wisdom and respect.

60. Ramona: is a Spanish name meaning "wise protector". It is a name associated with strength and guardianship.

61. Regina: is a Latin name meaning "queen". It is a name associated with royalty and leadership.

62. Rosalind: is a combination of the names Rose and Linda, meaning "beautiful rose". It is a name associated with grace and beauty.

63. Rosamund: is a Germanic name meaning "horse protection". It is a name associated with strength and loyalty.

64. Rosetta: is an Italian name meaning "little rose". It is a name associated with delicacy and sweetness.

65. Rowena: is a Welsh name meaning "famous joy". It is a name associated with happiness and fame.

66. Sabrina: is a Celtic name meaning "from the boundary river". It is a name associated with mystery and enchantment.

67. Selma: is a Germanic name meaning "helmet of God". It is a name associated with protection and strength.

68. Sybil: is a Greek name meaning "prophetess" or "oracle". It is a name associated with wisdom and foresight.

69. Thelma: is a Greek name meaning "will" or "wish". It is a name associated with

determination and desire.

70. Theodora: is a Greek name meaning "gift of God". It is a name associated with divine blessings and grace.

71. Trudy: is a diminutive of the name Gertrude, meaning "spear of strength". It is a name associated with resilience and power.

72. Ursula: is a Latin name meaning "little bear". It is a name associated with courage and protection.

73. Veda: is a Sanskrit name meaning "knowledge" or "sacred wisdom". It is a name associated with enlightenment and spirituality.

74. Velma: is a German name meaning "resolute protector". It is a name associated with strength and determination.

75. Vera: is a Russian name meaning "faith". It is a name associated with trust and loyalty.

76. Verity: is an English name meaning "truth". It is a name associated with honesty and integrity.

77. Viola: is a Latin name meaning "violet". It is a name associated with beauty and grace.

78. Virginia: is a Latin name meaning "pure" or "virgin". It is a name associated with purity and innocence.

79. Vivienne: is a French name meaning "alive" or "lively". It is a name associated with vitality and energy.

80. Winifred: is an English name meaning "blessed peace". It is a name associated with tranquility and harmony.

81. Wren: is an English name derived from the small bird. It is a name associated with freedom and agility.

82. Yvonne: is a French name meaning "yew tree". It is a name associated with strength and endurance.

83. Zelda: is a Yiddish name meaning "blessed" or "happy". It is a name associated with joy and good fortune.

84. Zelma: is a German name meaning "helmet of protection". It is a name associated with strength and defense.

Badass Princess Names

1. Aella: is a Greek name derived from the word "Aellô," which means a whirlwind or a storm. Aella is the name of an Amazon warrior who was known for wielding a double axe and was killed by Herakles in Greek mythology.

2. Althea: is a Greek name that means "healer". It is also a female biblical Greek name. The name Althea comes from the Greek word "althos," which means "healing power."

3. Ambrosia: is a Greek name that means "immortal" or "divine". Ambrosia is the food or drink of the gods in Greek mythology, and it is thought to confer immortality.

4. Anastasia: a Greek name that means "resurrection" It comes from the Greek word "anastasis," which means "rebirth." Anastasia is a popular name in Russian culture as well.

5. Andromeda: is a Greek name that means "ruler of men." Andromeda was a princess in Greek mythology who was saved from a sea monster by the hero Perseus.

6. Araminta: is an unpronounceable name, possibly derived from the Greek name "Artemis." It's also a popular name among African-Americans.

7. Artemis: is a Greek name that means "goddess of hunting." Artemis is Apollo's twin sister in Greek mythology, and she is associated with the moon, hunting, and wild animals.

8. Astra: is a Latin name that means "star". The term "Astrum" is derived from the Latin word "Astrum". Astra is also a well-known character in science fiction and fantasy literature.

9. Astrid: is a Scandinavian name that means "divinely beautiful". It is derived from the Old Norse words "as" (god) and "fridr" (beautiful). In Scandinavia, Astrid is a popular name.

10. Augustina: a Latin name that means "majestic" or "venerable". The word "augustus" is derived from the Latin word "augustus". Augustina is the feminine form of Augustus.

11. Aurora: is a Latin name that means "dawn". Aurora is the goddess of the dawn in Roman mythology. Aurora is a popular name in Spanish-speaking countries as well.

12. Beatrix: is a Latin name that means "she who brings joy." It comes from the Latin word "beatus," which means "happy." Beatrix is a spelling variation of Beatrice.

13. Briar: is a name that means "thorny bush" in English. The term "brer" is derived from the Old English word "brer".Briar is also linked to the fairy tale "Sleeping Beauty," in which the princess's name is Briar Rose.

14. Brielle: is a French name that means "God is my strength". The word "brielle" is derived from the French word "brielle". Brielle is a nickname for Gabrielle.

15. Calista: is a Greek name that means "most beautiful". The word "kalos" means "beautiful" in Greek. Calista is another spelling of Callista.

16. Calliope: is a Greek name that means "beautiful voice". Calliope is the muse of epic poetry and eloquence in Greek mythology. Calliope is a well-known name in the arts and literature.

17. Celestina: a Latin name that means "heavenly". The word "caelestis" means "heavenly" in Latin. Celestina is the feminine form of Celestine.

18. Cordelia: is a Celtic name that means "sea-daughter." It is derived from the Celtic words "cor" (daughter) and "delia" (sea). Cordelia appears in Shakespeare's play "King Lear."

19. Cressida :is a Greek name that means "gold". The word "chrysos" means "gold" in Greek. Cressida appears in Shakespeare's play "Troilus and Cressida."

20. Dahlia: is a Scandinavian name that means "valley". It comes from the Swedish word "dal," which means "valley." Dahlia is the name of a flower as well.

21. Danica: is a Slavic name that means "morning star". It is derived from the Slavic word "dan," which means "day".

22. Demetria: is a Greek name that means "follower of Demeter". Demeter is the goddess of agriculture and fertility in Greek mythology.

23. Elara: is a Greek name that means "bright". Elara is a mortal lover of Zeus who was later transformed into a constellation in Greek mythology.

24. Electra: is a Greek name that means "amber". Electra is the daughter of Agamemnon and Clytemnestra in Greek mythology.

25. Elowen: is a Cornish name that means "elm tree." It comes from the Cornish word "elvan," which means "elm".

26. Elysia: is a Greek name that means "blissful". In Greek mythology, Elysium is the afterlife paradise of the blessed.

27. Ember: is a name that means "spark" in English. It is derived from the Old English word "aemyrge," which means "spark".

28. Evangeline: is a Greek name that means "good news". It derives from the Greek words "EU" (for "good") and "angelos" (for "messenger").

29. Fallon: is an Irish name that means "leader". It is a corruption of the Irish word "fál," which means "ruler."

30. Felicity: is a Latin name that means "happiness." It comes from the Latin word "felicitas," which means "good luck."

31. Fierce: is a word that means "intense" in English. It is a name that is frequently used to convey strength and power.

32. Freya: is a Scandinavian name that means "lady". Freya is the goddess of love, fertility, and war in Norse mythology.

33. Gaia: is a Greek name that means "earth". Gaia is the goddess of the earth in Greek mythology.

34. Galadriel: is a fictional name created by J.R.R. Tolkien for his "Lord of the Rings" series. It is derived from the Sindarin words "galad" and "riel" which mean "radiant" and "maiden" respectively.

35. Genevieve: is a French name that means "people's woman." It is derived from the Germanic words "kuni" (kin) and "weo" (woman).

36. Guinevere: is a Welsh name that means "white phantom". Guinevere is King Arthur's queen in Arthurian legend.

37. Gwendolyn: is a Welsh name that means "white ring". It is derived from the Welsh words "gwen" (white) and "dolen" (ring).

38. Hera: is a Greek name that means "queen of the gods." Hera is the goddess of marriage and childbirth in Greek mythology.

39. Hermione: is a Greek name that means "messenger". Hermione is the daughter of King Menelaus and Queen Helen of Sparta in Greek mythology.

40. Inara: is an ambiguous name, possibly derived from the Hittite goddess Inara. In Arabic-speaking countries, it is also a popular name.

41. Indira: is a Sanskrit name that means "beauty". The word "indu" means "moon" in Sanskrit.

42. Isabeau: is a French name that means "God is my oath". It is a spelling variation of the name Isabel.

43. Jinx: is an English name that means "spell". It is frequently used as a name to convey mischief or playfulness.

44. Jocasta: is a Greek name that means "shining moon". Jocasta is Oedipus' mother and wife in Greek mythology.

45. Juniper: is a name that means "youth-producing" in English. It comes from the Latin word juniperus, which means "juniper tree."

46. Kallista: is a Greek name that means "most beautiful". The word "kalos" means "beautiful" in Greek.

47. Katarina: is a Slavic name that means "pure". It is a spelling variation of Katherine.

48. Kismet: is a Turkish name that means "fate". It is frequently used as a name to imply fate or inevitability.

49. Lark: is an English name meaning "songbird". It's a popular name for people who want to convey a sense of lightness or joy.

50. Lavinia: is a Latin name that means "purity". Lavinia is the daughter of King Latinus and the wife of Aeneas in Roman mythology.

51. Lenora: is a Greek name that means "light". It is a spelling variation of the name Eleanor.

52. Lilith: is a Hebrew name that means "night monster". Lilith is a demon who is thought to be Adam's first wife in Jewish mythology.

53. Liora: is a Hebrew name that means "my light." It comes from the Hebrew word "or," which means "light."

54. Lorelei: is a German name that translates as "alluring enchantress." Lorelei is a siren in German mythology who lures sailors to their deaths.

55. Magnolia: is a name that means "magnol's flower" in English. It is named after French botanist Pierre Magnol.

56. Marcella: is a Latin name that means "warlike". It is a female version of the name Marcellus.

57. Maven: means "expert" in Yiddish.

58. Morgana: is a French name derived from the Welsh name Morgan, which means "sea-circle." Morgana is a sorceress and King Arthur's half-sister in Arthurian legend.

59. Morrigan: is an Irish name that means "phantom queen". Morrigan is a goddess of battle, fate, and death in Irish mythology.

60. Niamh: is an Irish name that means "bright" or "radiant". Niamh is a goddess in Irish mythology and the daughter of the sea god Manannan.

61. Nixie: is a German name that means "water sprite." Nixies are water spirits who live in rivers and streams in German folklore.

62. Nyx: is a Greek name that means "night". Nyx is the goddess of the night in Greek mythology.

63. Octavia: is a Latin name that means "eighth".

64. Odessa: is a Greek name that means "long journey." It is also the name of a Ukrainian city.

65. Onyx: is a Greek name that means "claw" or "fingernail". It is a type of black gemstone as well.

66. Ophelia: is a Greek name that means "help" or "aid". It is also a character name in Shakespeare's play "Hamlet."

67. Pandora: is a Greek name that means "all-gifted". Pandora was the first woman created by the gods in Greek mythology, and she was given a box containing all the world's evils.

68. Persephone: A Greek name that means "bringer of destruction." Persephone is the underworld queen in Greek mythology and the daughter of Zeus and Demeter.

69. Phoenix: is a Greek name that means "dark red". The phoenix is a bird that is reborn from its ashes in Greek mythology.

70. Ravenna: Ravenna is an Italian name that means "raven". It's also the name of an Italian city famous for its Byzantine mosaics.

71. Rhiannon: is a Welsh name that means "great queen". Rhiannon is a Welsh goddess associated with horses and the underworld.

72. Rogue: is a name that means "vagabond" in English. It is also a term for someone dishonest or unprincipled.

73. Rosalind: is a Latin name that means "pretty rose". It is also a character name in Shakespeare's play "As You Like It."

74. Rowena: is a German name that means "famous friend." It is also a character name in Sir Walter Scott's novel "Ivanhoe."

75. Sabine: is a Latin name that means "woman from the Sabine tribe." The Sabines were a tribe of people who lived near Rome in Roman mythology.

76. Sapphira: is a Greek name that means "sapphire". Sapphira is Ananias' wife in the Bible, and she is known for lying to the apostles.

77. Selene: is a Greek name that means "moon". Selene is the goddess of the moon in Greek mythology.

78. Serafina: a Hebrew name that means "burning one" The seraphim are the highest order of angels in Christianity.

79. Seraphina: is a Hebrew name that means "the fiery ones." The seraphim are the highest order of angels in Christianity.

80. Seren: is a Welsh name that means "star". It's also the name of a character on the British television show "Doctor Who."

81. Talia: is a Hebrew name that means "God's dew." Talia is the name of a princess who falls into a deep sleep and is awakened by a prince's kiss in Italian folklore.

82. Thalia: is a Greek name that means "to blossom." Thalia is one of the nine muses in Greek mythology and the goddess of comedy and pastoral poetry.

83. Theodora: is a Greek name that means "God's gift." It's also the name of several Byzantine empresses.

84. Valentina: is a Latin name that means "strong, healthy". It is also the name of a martyred saint for her faith.

85. Valkyrie: is a Norse name that means "slain chooser." The Valkyries are female warriors in Norse mythology who choose which warriors will die in battle and be taken to Valhalla.

86. Veda: is a Sanskrit name that means "knowledge". The Vedas are the oldest sacred texts in Hinduism.

87. Vesper: is a Latin name that means "evening star". It's also a character name in Ian Fleming's James Bond novel "Casino Royale."

88. Vespera: is a Latin name that means "evening". It is also the name of a moth genus.

89. Xanthe: is a Greek name that means "yellow". In Greek mythology, Xanthe is the name of one of the Oceanids, the Titan Oceanus' daughters.

90. Xena: is a Greek name that means "guest". It is also the name of a character in the television series "Xena: Warrior Princess."

91. Yara: is a Brazilian name that means "water lady". Yara is a mermaid-like creature who lives in the Amazon River in Brazilian folklore.

92. Zahara: is a Hebrew name that means "flower". It is also the name of a Moroccan city.

93. Zenobia: is a Greek name that means "life of Zeus". Zenobia was a queen of the Palmyrene Empire in Syria during the Middle Ages.

94. Zephyra: is a Greek name that means "west wind".

Strong Names

1. Ada: is a Germanic name that means "noble" or "nobility". It is a timeless and classic name.

2. Alexandra: is a Greek name that means "defender of humanity." It's a commanding and regal name.

3. Amira: an Arabic name that means "princess" or "commander". It's a lovely and exotic name.

4. Aria: Aria is an Italian name that means "air" or "song". It's a lovely and elegant name.

5. Astrid: a Scandinavian name that means "divinely beautiful." It's a one-of-a-kind and endearing name.

6. Athena: A Greek name that means "goddess of wisdom and war." It's a strong and uplifting name.

7. Bellatrix: a Latin name that means "female warrior." It's a strong and commanding name.

8. Bree: is an Irish name that means "strength" or "virtue". It's a short and simple name.

9. Briana: is an Irish name that means "strong" or "virtuous". It is a contemporary and feminine name.

10. Brielle: is a French name that means "God is my strength." It's a lovely and graceful name.

11. Cadence: is a Latin word that means "rhythm" or "flow". It's a memorable and musical name.

12. Calista: is a Greek name that means "most beautiful" or "most lovely". It's a refined and elegant name.

13. Calliope: a Greek name that means "beautiful voice." It's a beautiful and artistic name.

14. Celeste: a Latin name that means "heavenly" or "of the sky." It is a divine and ethereal name.

15. Celestia: is a Latin name that means "heavenly" or "of the sky." It's a one-of-a-kind and enchanting name.

16. Dahlia: is the name of a flower derived from the dahlia plant. It represents elegance, dignity, and grace.

17. Danica: a Slavic name that means "morning star" It's a bright and shining name.

18. Darcy: is a French name that means "from Arcy" or "dark one." It's a unisex name with literary overtones.

19. Delaney: is an Irish name that means "from the alder grove." It is a trendy and modern name.

20. Dominique: is a French name that means "belonging to the Lord." It's a unisex name with a strong, confident ring to it.

21. Elara: is a Greek name that means "bright" or "shining". It is a divine and mystical name.

22. Eleanor: is a Greek name that means "bright" or "shining one". It is a timeless and classic name.

23. Elowen: is a Cornish name that means "elm tree." It's a one-of-a-kind name inspired by nature.

24. Ember: is an English name that means "spark" or "burning low". It is a passionate and fiery name.

25. Emery: is a German name that means "hardworking leader." It's a strong and modern-sounding unisex name.

26. Esme: is a French name that means "esteemed" or "loved." It's a lovely and romantic name.

27. Evangeline: is a Greek name that means "bearer of good news." It's a lovely and poetic name.

28. Everly: is an English name that means "from the boar meadow." It is a trendy and modern name.

29. Fallon: an Irish name that means "leader" or "superior one." It's a unisex name with a strong, confident ring to it.

30. Fiona: is a Scottish name that means "fair" or "white." It's a lovely and timeless name.

31. Freya: is a Scandinavian name that translates as "goddess of love, fertility, and war." It's a strong and mystical name.

32. Genevieve: is a French name that means "woman of the people." It's a refined and elegant name.

33. Giselle: is a French name that means "pledge" or "oath." It's a lovely and romantic name.

34. Gwendolyn: is a Welsh name that means "white ring" or "blessed ring." It's a commanding and regal name.

35. Harper: is an English name that means "harp player." It is a trendy and modern name.

36. Haven: is an English name that means "a haven or refuge." It's a calm and serene name.

37. Imara: is a Swahili name that means "strong" or "firm." It's a one-of-a-kind and exotic name.

38. Ingrid: is a Scandinavian name that means "fair and lovely." It's a timeless and elegant name.

39. Isla: is a Scottish name that means "island." It's a short and sweet name.

40. Isolde: is a German name that means "ice ruler." It's a one-of-a-kind and enigmatic name.

41. Jocelyn: a French name that means "joyous". It's a lovely and feminine name.

42. Juniper: is a Latin name that means "youth producing" or "evergreen." It is a trendy and nature-inspired name.

43. Juno: a Latin name that means "queen of the heavens" It is a commanding and regal name.

44. Kaia: is a Hawaiian name that means "sea" or "ocean". It's a lovely and exotic name.

45. Katarina: a Greek name that means "pure". It is a timeless and classic name.

46. Kiera: is an Irish name that means "dark-haired". It is a contemporary and feminine name.

47. Lark: is an English name that means "songbird." It's a one-of-a-kind name inspired by nature.

48. Leona: is a Latin name that means "lioness." It's a strong and intimidating name.

49. Lila: is a Persian name that means "night". It's a lovely and graceful name.

50. Lorelei: is a German name that means "alluring enchantress." It's a mystical and romantic story.

51. Luna: is a Latin name that means "moon". It's a magical and celestial name.

52. Lyra: is a Greek name that means "lyre" or "harp". It's a beautiful and poetic name.

53. Magnolia: is a Latin name that means "magnolia's flower." It's a lovely, nature-inspired name.

54. Marcella: is a Latin name that means "warlike". It's a powerful and feminine

55. Maxine: is a Latin name that means "greatest". It is a contemporary and powerful name.

56. Mira: is a Latin name that means "wonderful" or "admirable". It's a short and sweet name.

57. Nadia: is a Russian name that means "hope". It's a lovely and feminine name.

58. Nola: is an Irish name that means "famous" or "fair shoulder". It's a one-of-a-kind and endearing name.

59. Nova: a Latin name that means "new" It is a trendy and modern name.

60. Octavia: is a Latin name that means "eighth". It's a commanding and regal name.

61. Odette: is a French name that means "wealthy" or "prosperous". It's a lovely and elegant name.

62. Ophelia: is a Greek name that means "help" or "aid". It's a lovely and poetic name.

63. Petra: is a Greek name that means "rock" or "stone". It's a strong and distinct name.

64. Phoenix: a Greek name that means "dark red" It's a strong and mythical name.

65. Piper: is an English name that means "flute player." It's a lively and spunky name.

66. Quinn: is an Irish name that means "wise" or "intelligent". It is a strong and contemporary unisex name.

67. Raina: is a Slavic name that means "queen" or "pure". It's a lovely and distinct name.

68. Raine: is a French name that means "queen" or "pure". It's a straightforward and elegant name.

69. Raven: is a name that means "blackbird" in English. It's a mysterious and edgy name.

70. Reagan: is an Irish name that means "little king." It's a strong and contemporary name.

71. Rosalind: is a Latin name that means "pretty rose". It is a traditional and romantic name.

72. Rosalyn: a Latin name that means "pretty rose" It is a contemporary and feminine name.

73. Rowan: a Gaelic name that means "little red one" It is a masculine and nature-inspired unisex name.

Virtue Names

1. Amity: is a name that means "friendship" or "harmony" in English. It is a name connected with harmony and tranquility.

2. Bliss: is an English word name that means "extreme happiness" or "joy". It is a name connected with joy and fulfillment.

3. Charity: a name that means "generosity" or "kindness" in English. It is a name linked with kindness and generosity.

4. Compassion: is a term in English that means "sympathy" or "empathy." It is a name connected with empathy and concern for others.

5. Constance: a name that means "steadfastness" or "faithfulness" in English. It is a name linked with dependability and commitment.

6. Courage: is a name in English that means "bravery" or "fearlessness." It is a name connected with fortitude and perseverance.

7. Destiny: an English word name that means "fate" or "fortune." It is a name that is associated with a specific destiny or goal.

8. Diligence: is a name in English that means "hard work" or "perseverance." It's a name connected with hard work and tenacity.

9. Faith: is an English word name that means "belief" or "trust". It is a name that is associated with strong religious or spiritual beliefs.

10. Felicity: is an English name that means "happiness" or "good fortune". It is a name connected with happiness and optimism.

11. Forgiveness: an English word meaning "pardoning" or "letting go of resentment". It is a name that connotes kindness and compassion.

12. Gentleness: is a name in English that means "kindness" or "tenderness." It is a name connected with a kind and nurturing personality.

13. Grace: is an English name that means "elegance" or "divine favor". It's a name synonymous with beauty and charm.

14. Gracious: is a name in English that means "courteous" or "kind." It is a name that is connected with courtesy and charity.

15. Harmony: is a name in English that means "agreement" or "peaceful balance." It is a name linked with peace and harmony.

16. Honesty: is a name in English that means "truthfulness" or "integrity." It is a

name linked with sincerity and dependability.

17. Honor: is an English word name that means "respect" or "high regard." It is a name connected with respect and dignity.

18. Hope: is an English word name that means "optimism" or "desire for a positive outcome." It is a name connected with hope and ambition.

19. Humility: is a name in English that means "modesty" or "lack of arrogance." It's a name that connotes modesty and humility.

20. Innocence: is an English word name that means "purity" or "liberation from guilt." It's a name linked with innocence and naivete.

21. Joy: is a name that means "happiness" or "delight" in English. It is a name connected with joy and celebration.

22. Justice: is an English word that denotes fairness, righteousness, and the moral rightness principle.

23. Kindness: is an English word meaning compassion, generosity, and the attribute of being kind and considerate.

24. Liberty: is an English word name that denotes freedom, independence, and the state of being liberated from oppressive constraints.

25. Loving: is an English term meaning compassion, caring, and the act of showing love and tenderness.

26. Loyalty: an English word meaning fidelity, commitment, and the attribute of being true and committed to someone or something.

27. Mercy: is an English word meaning compassion, forgiveness, and the act of being kind and lenient to others.

28. Modesty: is an English word meaning humility, simplicity, and the quality of not being overly proud or boastful.

29. Patience: is an English word meaning endurance, tolerance, and the ability to stay cool and composed in tough conditions.

30. Peace: is an English word meaning tranquillity, harmony, and the absence of conflict or violence.

31. Prudence: is an English word that signifies knowledge, caution, and the capacity to make sound and deliberate decisions.

32. Purity: is an English word meaning innocence, cleanliness, and the state of being free of impurities or moral corruption.

33. Radiance: an English word meaning brightness, attractiveness, and the attribute of gleaming or glowing with light.

34. Serenity: is an English word meaning stillness, tranquillity, and the state of being serene and undisturbed.

35. Sincerity: is an English word meaning authenticity, honesty, and the trait of being truthful and sincere in one's acts and statements.

36. Temperance: is an English word meaning self-control, moderation, and the ability to refrain from excess or extremes.

37. Truth: is an English word meaning honesty, authenticity, and the trait of adhering to fact or reality.

38. Understanding: is an English word for empathy, comprehension, and the ability to grasp or comprehend ideas and feelings.

39. Unity: is an English word meaning "togetherness," "harmony," and "the state of being united or joined as one."

40. Valor: is an English word name that denotes bravery, courage, and the trait of displaying great fortitude and tenacity in the face of danger or hardship.

41. Verity: is an English term meaning truth, honesty, and the attribute of being true or genuine.

42. Wisdom: is an English word meaning knowledge, insight, and the capacity to make smart decisions based on experience and understanding.

Literary Names

1. Agatha: is derived from the Old Greek word "agathos," which means "good" and "kind." It was made famous by a Christian martyr from the third century who became the patron saint of nurses. Agatha is a traditional name that can be abbreviated to "Aggie" for a more modern feel.

2. Agnes: is an English version of a Greek name that means "chaste." It was a popular name in the late 1800s but has since declined in popularity. Agnes is a classic and timeless name with religious connotations.

3. Alice: is an English girl's name that means "noble" or "of noble kind." It is a traditional name that has been in use for centuries. Lewis Carroll, the author of Alice in Wonderland, and actress Alice Eve are both famous bearers of the name.

4. Antigone: is a Greek name that means "against birth" or "in place of a parent". Antigone was the daughter of Oedipus and Jocasta in Greek mythology. She is well-known for her devotion and defiance of authority.

5. Araminta: has an uncertain meaning and is of English origin. It is a distinct and uncommon name that rose to prominence in the 18th century. Araminta is a beautiful and feminine name.

6. Ariel: is a Hebrew name that means "God's lion." It's a unisex name made popular by the character Ariel in Disney's "The Little Mermaid." Ariel has a whimsical and magical atmosphere.

7. Arwen: is a Welsh name that means "noble maiden." It rose to prominence as a result of the character Arwen in J.R.R. Tolkien's "The Lord of the Rings" series. Arwen is a lovely and ethereal name.

8. Arya: is a Sanskrit name that means "noble" or "honorable". It rose to prominence as a result of the character Arya Stark in the HBO series "Game of Thrones." Arya is a powerful and contemporary name.

9. Beatrice: is a Latin name that means "she who brings happiness" or "blessed". It is a traditional and timeless name that has been in use for centuries. Author Beatrice Potter Webb and actress Beatrice Arthur are both famous bearers of the name.

10. Briony: is an English name derived from the name of a flowering vine. It rose to prominence as a result of the character Briony Tallis in Ian McEwan's novel "Atonement." Briony is a one-of-a-kind, nature-inspired name.

11. Catherine: is a Greek name that means "pure" or "clear". It is a traditional and timeless name that has been in use for centuries. Catherine the Great of Russia and actress Catherine Zeta-Jones are two famous bearers of the name.

12. Celia: is a Latin name that means "heavenly" or "celestial". It is an elegant and feminine name that has been used since antiquity. Celia's voice is delicate and graceful.

13. Charlotte: is a French name that means "free man" or "little one." It is a traditional and elegant name that has been in use for centuries. Charlotte Bronte, author, and Princess Charlotte of Cambridge are famous bearers of the name.

14. Cordelia: is a Celtic name that means "heart" or "daughter of the sea." It rose to prominence as a result of the character Cordelia in Shakespeare's play "King Lear." Cordelia is an evocative and poetic name.

15. Cosette: a French name that means "victorious people" It rose to prominence as a result of the character Cosette in Victor Hugo's novel "Les Misérables." Cosette has a delicate and romantic tone to it.

16. Cosima: is an Italian name that means "order" or "harmony." It rose to prominence as a result of the character Cosima Niehaus in the television series "Orphan Black." Cosima is a one-of-a-kind and artistic name.

17. Cressida: This Greek name means "gold." It rose to prominence as a result of the character Cressida in Shakespeare's play "Troilus and Cressida." Cressida is a powerful and sophisticated name.

18. Darcy: is a French name that means "from Arcy" or "dark one." It rose to prominence as a result of the character Mr. Darcy in Jane Austen's novel "Pride and Prejudice." Darcy is a unisex name with a sophisticated and timeless vibe.

19. Desdemona: is a Greek word that means "ill-fated" or "unlucky." It rose to prominence as a result of the character Desdemona in Shakespeare's play "Othello." Desdemona is an ominous and tragic name.

20. Edith: is of Old English origin and means "prosperous in war" or "riches". It is a traditional and timeless name that has been popular throughout history. Edith Wharton, the Pulitzer Prize-winning author, and Edith Piaf, the French singer, are both famous bearers of the name.

21. Elinor: is an English name that means "God is my light" or "shining light." It rose to prominence as a result of the character Elinor Dashwood in Jane Austen's novel "Sense and Sensibility." Elinor is a classic and sophisticated name.

22. Eliza: is a Hebrew name that means "God is my oath." It is a diminutive of Elizabeth and gained popularity as a result of the character Eliza Doolittle in the musical "My Fair Lady." Eliza is a vibrant and endearing name.

23. Emma: is a Germanic name that means "universal" or "complete." It is a traditional and timeless name that has been in use for centuries. Author Jane Austen and actress Emma Watson are two famous bearers of the name.

24. Eowyn: is an Old English name that means "horse joy" or "horse lover." It rose

to prominence as a result of the character Eowyn in J.R.R. Tolkien's "The Lord of the Rings" series. Eowyn is a courageous and strong name.

25. Esme: is a French word that means "esteemed" or "loved." It rose to prominence as a result of the character Esme Cullen in the "Twilight" series. Esme is a lovely and refined name.

26. Esmeralda: is of Spanish origin and means "emerald". It rose to prominence as a result of the character Esmeralda in Victor Hugo's novel "The Hunchback of Notre Dame." Esmeralda is a captivating and exotic name.

27. Estella: is a Spanish name that means "star". It rose to prominence as a result of the character Estella in Charles Dickens's novel "Great Expectations." Estella is a lovely and celestial name.

28. Evangeline: is a Greek name that means "bearer of good news." It is a feminine and elegant name with a religious meaning. A poem by Henry Wadsworth Longfellow is also called Evangeline.

29. Fantin: is a French name with an unknown meaning. It rose to prominence as a result of the character Fantine in Victor Hugo's novel "Les Misérables." Fantine is a one-of-a-kind and dramatic name.

30. Fleur: a French name that means "flower" It is a delicate and feminine name associated with nature and beauty. Fleur is also the name of a character in the "Harry Potter" series by J.K. Rowling.

31. Flora: is a Latin name that means "flower". It is named after the Roman goddess of spring and flowers. Flora is a classic and sophisticated name.

32. Francine: is a French name that means "free". It is a feminine form of the name Francis that sounds sophisticated and chic. Francine is a timeless and classic name.

33. Gemma: is a Latin name that means "gem" or "precious stone." It is a beautiful and rare name that is feminine and elegant. Gemma is also a saint's name.

34. Georgiana: a feminine form of George that means "farmer" or "earth-worker." It rose to prominence as a result of the character Georgiana Darcy in Jane Austen's novel "Pride and Prejudice." Georgiana is a regal and refined name.

35. Ginevra: is an Italian name that means "white shadow" or "fair one". It is the Italian form of the name Guinevere and became popular as a result of J.K. Rowling's "Harry Potter" character Ginevra Weasley. Ginevra is a one-of-a-kind and enchanting name.

36. Guinevere: is a Welsh name that means "white phantom" or "fair one." Guinevere was King Arthur's queen in Arthurian legend. Guinevere is a mythical and romantic name.

37. Gwendolen: is a Welsh name that means "white ring" or "fair bow." It rose to

prominence as a result of the character Gwendolen Fairfax in Oscar Wilde's play "The Importance of Being Earnest." Gwendolen is a powerful and sophisticated name.

38. Hedwig: is a Germanic name that means "battle" or "strife". It rose to prominence as a result of the character Hedwig in J.K. Rowling's "Harry Potter" series. Hedwig is a whimsical and unusual name.

39. Hermione: is a Greek name that means "messenger" or "earthly". It rose to prominence as a result of the character Hermione Granger in J.K. Rowling's "Harry Potter" series. Hermione is a powerful and wise name.

40. Hero: is a Greek name that means "heroic" or "defender." It rose to prominence as a result of the character Hero in William Shakespeare's play "Much Ado About Nothing." Hero is a strong and commanding name.

41. Imelda: comes from the Germanic language and means "universal battle" or "whole battle." It rose to prominence as a result of Saint Imelda, an Italian saint known for her piety and devotion. Imelda is a distinct and powerful name.

42. Imogen: is a Celtic name that means "maiden" or "innocent". It rose to prominence as a result of the character Imogen in Shakespeare's play "Cymbeline." Imogen is a classic and sophisticated name.

43. Isabella: is a Hebrew name that means "God is my oath." It is a feminine form of Isabel that has been in use for centuries. Isabella is a traditional and romantic name.

44. Isadora: is a Greek name that means "gift of Isis." It rose to prominence as a result of the dancer Isadora Duncan, who was known for her innovative and expressive style. Isadora is a distinctive and artistic name.

45. Isolde: is a Celtic name that means "ice ruler" or "ice ruler." Isolde was a tragic heroine in Arthurian legend who fell in love with Tristan. The name Isolde is both romantic and mythical.

46. Jane: is an English name that means "God Is gracious." It is a feminine version of the name John that has been in use for centuries. Jane is a timeless and classic name.

47. Juliet: is a French name that means "youthful". It rose to prominence as a result of the character Juliet in Shakespeare's play "Romeo and Juliet." Juliet is a lovely and romantic name.

48. Katniss: a Greek name that means "night-blooming flower" It rose to prominence as a result of the character Katniss Everdeen in Suzanne Collins's "The Hunger Games" series. Katniss Everdeen has a strong and independent name.

49. Lavinia: a Latin name that means "purity" or "woman of Rome". It rose to prominence as a result of the character Lavinia in Shakespeare's play "Titus

Andronicus." Lavinia is a traditional and elegant name.

50. Lyra: is a Greek name that means "lyre" or "musical instrument". It rose to prominence as a result of the character Lyra Belacqua in Philip Pullman's "His Dark Materials" series. Lyra is a memorable and beautiful name.

51. Lysandra: is a Greek name that means "liberator of men." It is a feminine form of the name Lysander with a powerful and empowering sound. Lysandra is a one-of-a-kind and powerful name.

52. Marianne: is a name derived from the names Mary and Anne, and it means "bitter grace" or "graceful one." It rose to prominence as a result of the character Marianne Dashwood in Jane Austen's novel "Sense and Sensibility." Marianne is a traditional and romantic name.

53. Matilda: is a Germanic name that means "mighty in battle." It rose to prominence as a result of the character Matilda Wormwood in Roald Dahl's novel "Matilda." Matilda is a powerful and tenacious name.

54. Meg: is a Greek name that means "pearl". It is a diminutive of Margaret, and it has a simple and timeless sound. Meg is a timeless and sophisticated name.

55. Megara: is a Greek name that means "pearl". It rose to prominence as a result of the character Megara in Disney's "Hercules."

56. Miranda: is a Latin name that means "adorable" or "wonderful." It rose to prominence as a result of the character Miranda in Shakespeare's play "The Tempest." Miranda is a timeless and sophisticated name.

57. Nora: is a Latin name that means "honor" or "light". It is a diminutive of Eleanor and has been used for centuries. Nora is a classic and sophisticated name.

58. Octavia: is a Latin name that means "eighth". It was traditionally given to a family's eighth child. Octavia is a regal and refined name.

59. Odette: is a French name that means "wealthy" or "prosperous". It rose to prominence as the character Odette in Tchaikovsky's ballet "Swan Lake." Odette is a lovely and refined name.

60. Ophelia: is a Greek name that means "help" or "aid." It rose to prominence as a result of the character Ophelia in Shakespeare's play "Hamlet." Ophelia is a tragic and romantic name.

61. Penelope: is a Greek name that means "weaver" or "duck". It rose to prominence as a result of the character Penelope in Homer's epic poem "The Odyssey." Penelope is a traditional and elegant name.

62. Pippa: is a diminutive of Philippa, which means "horse lover." It gained popularity as a result of the Duchess of Cambridge's sister, Pippa Middleton. Pippa is a sweet and lively name.

63. Portia: is a Latin name that means "pig" or "doorkeeper". It rose to prominence as a result of the character Portia in Shakespeare's play "The Merchant of Venice." Portia is a powerful and wise name.

64. Primrose: a name that means "first rose" in English. It rose to prominence as a result of the character Primrose Everdeen in Suzanne Collins's "The Hunger Games" series. Primrose is a one-of-a-kind and whimsical name.

65. Rosalind: a Latin name that means "pretty rose" It rose to prominence as a result of the character Rosalind in Shakespeare's play "As You Like It." Rosalind is a traditional and romantic name.

66. Rosaline: is a Latin name that means "pretty rose". It rose to prominence as a result of the character Rosaline in Shakespeare's play "Romeo and Juliet." Rosaline is a lovely and romantic name.

67. Rosalyn: is a Latin name that means "pretty rose". It is a nickname for Rosalind and has a similar sound and meaning. Rosalyn is a timeless and classic name.

68. Rosamund: is a Germanic name that means "horse protection." It rose to prominence as a result of the character Rosamund Vincy in George Eliot's novel "Middlemarch." Rosamund is a powerful and sophisticated name.

69. Sabrina: is a Latin name that means "from the Severn River." It rose to prominence as a result of the character Sabrina in John Milton's poem "Comus." Sabrina is a mysterious and enticing name.

70. Saffron: a spice derived from the crocus flower, as well as an English girl's name. It is a distinctive and exotic name associated with luxury and sophistication.

71. Sapphira: is a Greek name that means "sapphire". It gained popularity as a result of the biblical character Sapphira. Sapphira is a one-of-a-kind and valuable name.

72. Scarlett: Scarlett is a name that means "red" in English. It rose to prominence as a result of the character Scarlett O'Hara in Margaret Mitchell's novel "Gone with the Wind." Scarlett is a strong, passionate name.

73. Scout: is a name that means "to listen" in English. It rose to prominence as a result of the character Scout Finch in Harper Lee's novel "To Kill a Mockingbird." Scout is a unique and daring name.

74. Sylvia: is a Latin name that means "from the forest." It rose to prominence as a result of the character Sylvia in Shakespeare's play "The Two Gentlemen of Verona." Sylvia is a timeless and sophisticated name.

75. Tess: is a diminutive of the name Theresa, which means "harvester" or "summer." It rose to prominence as a result of the character Tess Durbeyfield in Thomas Hardy's novel "Tess of the d'Urbervilles." Tess is a straightforward and timeless name.

76. Verity: is a Latin name that means "truth." It is a virtuous name with a powerful and empowering ring to it. Verity is a one-of-a-kind and meaningful name.

77. Viola: is a Latin name that means "violet". It rose to prominence as a result of the character Viola in Shakespeare's play "Twelfth Night." Viola is a traditional and romantic name.

78. Vivienne: a French name that means "alive" or "lively". It rose to prominence as a result of the character Vivienne in Arthurian legend. Vivienne is a refined and elegant name.

79. Wendy: is a name that means "friend" in English. It rose to prominence as a result of the character Wendy Darling in J.M. Barrie's novel "Peter Pan." Wendy is a sweet and welcoming name.

80. Winnie: is a diminutive of Winifred and means "blessed peacemaking." It rose to prominence as a result of the character Winnie-the-Pooh in A.A. Milne's children's books. Winnie is a sweet and playful name.

81. Zelda: a Yiddish name that means "blessed" It rose to prominence as a result of the video game character Zelda in the "Legend of Zelda" series. Zelda is a one-of-a-kind and mystical name.

Mythology Names

1. Acantha: a Greek name that means "thorn," given to a nymph in Greek mythology.

2. Adrasteia: Greek name meaning "inescapable," given to the goddess of vengeance who assisted in Zeus's birth.

3. Aine: An Irish name that means "brightness," and is the name of the goddess of love and summer in Irish mythology.

4. Alecto: Greek name meaning "unceasing," given to one of Greek mythology's Furies.

5. Althea: Greek name meaning "healer" or "wholesome," given to a Greek mythological queen who was turned into a plant.

6. Amaterasu: A Japanese name that means "shining heaven," given to the sun goddess in Japanese mythology.

7. Anahita: a Persian name that means "pure," given to the Persian goddess of fertility and water.

8. Ananke: Greek name meaning "necessity," given to the Greek goddess of inevitability and compulsion.

9. Andromeda: Greek name meaning "ruler of men," given to a princess who was chained to a rock in Greek mythology.

10. Anthea: Greek name meaning "flowery," given to a goddess associated with flowers and gardens in Greek mythology.

11. Aphrodite: Greek name meaning "risen from the foam," given to the Greek goddess of love, beauty, and pleasure.

12. Aradia: is an Italian name that means "queen of the witches," and it is the name of a legendary figure in Italian folklore and modern Wicca.

13. Arianrhod: Welsh name meaning "silver wheel," given to the Welsh goddess of the moon and stars.

14. Artemis: a Greek name that means "safe and sound," given to the Greek goddess of hunting, the wilderness, and childbirth.

15. Asherah: Hebrew name meaning "grove," given to a goddess of fertility and motherhood in ancient Near Eastern mythology.

16. Athena: Greek name meaning "wisdom," given to the Greek goddess of wisdom, strategic warfare, and crafts.

17. Atropos: Greek name meaning "unbending," borne by one of Greek mythology's three Fates who cut the thread of life.

18. Aurora: A Latin name meaning "dawn," given to the Roman goddess of the dawn.

19. Bastet: Egyptian name meaning "devourer," given to the Egyptian goddess of cats, fertility, and childbirth.

20. Bellona: Roman name meaning "war," given to the Roman goddess of war and destruction.

21. Branwen: A Welsh name meaning "blessed raven," given to a princess associated with love and beauty in Welsh mythology.

22. Brigid: is an Irish name that means "exalted one," and it is given to the goddess of fire, poetry, and wisdom in Celtic mythology.

23. Brizo: is the Greek goddess of sailors and seafarers.

24. Brynhildr: An Old Norse name meaning "armor-battle," given to a shieldmaiden in Norse mythology.

25. Calliope: Greek name meaning "beautiful voice," given to the Greek mythological muse of epic poetry.

26. Calypso: Greek name that means "to conceal," given to a nymph in Greek mythology who held Odysseus captive for seven years.

27. Camilla: is a Roman name that means "attendant of the temple," and was given to a warrior maiden in Roman mythology.

28. Cassandra: Greek name meaning "prophetess," given to a Greek mythological princess who was cursed to never be believed.

29. Ceres: Roman name meaning "to grow," given to the Roman goddess of agriculture, grain, and motherly love.

30. Circe: is a Greek name that means "bird," and it was given to a sorceress in Greek mythology who turned men into pigs.

31. Demeter: Greek name meaning "earth mother," given to the Greek goddess of agriculture, fertility, and harvest.

32. Dido: is a Phoenician name that means "wanderer," and it was given to the queen of Carthage in Greek mythology.

33. Echidna: a Greek name meaning "she-viper," given to a half-woman, half-snake monster from Greek mythology.

34. Eris: Greek name meaning "strife," given to the Greek goddess of discord and chaos.

35. Freya: Norse name meaning "lady," given to the Norse goddess of love, fertility, and war.

36. Frigg: Norse name meaning "beloved," given to the Norse goddess of marriage and motherhood.

37. Gaia: Greek name meaning "earth," given to the earth goddess and mother of all life in Greek mythology.

38. Gorgon: a Greek name that means "dreadful," given to three monster sisters in Greek mythology.

39. Hecate: Greek name meaning "far-reaching," given to the Greek goddess of magic, witchcraft, and crossroads.

40. Hera: Greek name meaning "queen," given to the Greek goddess of marriage, women, and childbirth.

41. Idun: Norse name meaning "rejuvenator," given to the Norse goddess of youth and vitality.

42. Iris: Greek name meaning "rainbow," given to the Greek goddess of the rainbow and messenger of the gods.

43. Jocasta: Greek name meaning "shining moon," given to Oedipus' mother and wife in Greek mythology.

44. Juno: Roman name meaning "queen of the heavens," given to the Roman mythological goddess of marriage, women, and childbirth.

45. Kali: Hindu name meaning "black," given to the Hindu goddess of destruction and creation.

46. Keres: Greek name meaning "death spirits," borne by the female Greek spirits of death and doom.

47. Lachesis: Greek name meaning "apportioner," given to the Greek goddess of fate and destiny.

48. Leda: a Greek name that means "happy," given to Tyndareus' wife and Helen of Troy in Greek mythology.

49. Medusa: Greek name meaning "guardian," given to a gorgon with serpents for hair who turned people to stone in Greek mythology.

50. Morrigan: An Irish name that means "phantom queen," given to the Celtic goddess of war and fate.

51. Niamh: an Irish name that means "bright," and is the name of the goddess of beauty and youth in Irish mythology.

52. Nike: Greek name meaning "victory," given to the Greek goddess of victory.

53. Ondine: A Latin name that means "little wave," and is carried by water nymphs in folklore and mythology.

54. Penelope: Greek name meaning "weaver," given to Odysseus's wife who waited for him for 20 years in Greek mythology.

55. Persephone: Greek name meaning "bringer of destruction," given to the Greek goddess of the underworld and spring growth.

56. Quetzalcoatl: Aztec name meaning "feathered serpent," borne by the Aztec god of wind, air, and learning.

57. Rhea: Greek name meaning "flowing stream," given to the Greek goddess of fertility, motherhood, and generation.

58. Rowena: is a Welsh name that means "fairy," and it was given to a legendary figure in Welsh mythology who was associated with wisdom and poetry.

59. Siren: Greek name meaning "entangler," given to dangerous creatures in Greek mythology who used their singing to lure sailors to their deaths.

60. Skadi: Norse name meaning "damage," borne by the Norse goddess of winter, mountains, and hunting.

61. Surya: Hindu name meaning "sun," given to the sun god in Hindu mythology.

62. Tara: is a Sanskrit name that means "star," and it is the name of a goddess in Hindu and Buddhist mythology who is associated with compassion and wisdom.

63. Thalia: Greek name meaning "to flourish," given to the Greek mythological muse of comedy and idyllic poetry.

64. Theia: Greek name meaning "divine," given to the Greek goddess of sight and brightness.

65. Urd: Norse name meaning "fate," given to one of the three Norns in Norse mythology who oversaw the fates of gods and mortals.

66. Valkyrie: A Norse name that means "chooser of the slain," given to female warriors in Norse mythology who chose the bravest dead to go to Valhalla.

67. Venus: a Roman name meaning "love," given to the Roman goddess of love, beauty, and fertility.

68. Wicca: An Old English name meaning "witch," given to a modern neo-pagan goddess associated with nature and magic.

69. Xochiquetzal: an Aztec name meaning "flower feather," given to the Aztec goddess of love, beauty, and fertility.

70. Yemaya: Yoruba name meaning "mother of fish," borne by the Yoruba goddess of the sea and motherhood.

Nature Names

1. Aria: is an Italian name that means "air" or "song". It rose to prominence as a result of the character Aria Montgomery in the television show "Pretty Little Liars." Aria is a lovely and musical name.

2. Aurora: a Latin name that means "dawn" It gained popularity as a result of the ancient goddess of the dawn. Aurora is a beautiful and mystical name.

3. Autumn: is an English name that means "harvest season." It is a botanical name that connotes warmth and abundance. Autumn is a lovely and natural name.

4. Azure: is a French name that means "sky blue". It is a one-of-a-kind and exotic name associated with the color blue.

5. Blossom: an English name that means "flower" It's a botanical name that means "beauty and growth." Blossom is a sweet and playful name.

6. Briar: is an English name that means "thorny bush." It rose to prominence as a result of the character Briar Rose in the fairy tale "Sleeping Beauty." Briar is a one-of-a-kind and natural name.

7. Brooke: an English name that means "stream" It is a nature name associated with serenity and peace. Brooke is a straightforward and elegant name.

8. Clementine: is a French name that means "merciful". It rose to prominence as a result of the folk song "Oh My Darling, Clementine." Clementine is a sweet and lively name.

9. Clover: is an English name that means "meadow flower." It is a botanical name associated with good fortune and prosperity. Clover is a sweet and playful name.

10. Coral: is a Latin name that means "coral". It is a natural name related to the ocean and marine life. Coral is a distinctive and exotic name.

11. Crystal: a Greek name that means "ice" or "clear". It became popular because of the gemstone crystal. The name Crystal is mystical and enchanting.

12. Dahlia: is a Scandinavian name that means "valley". It is a botanical name that connotes beauty and elegance. Dahlia is a lovely and natural name.

13. Daisy: is a name that means "day's eye" in English. It is a botanical name that connotes innocence and purity. Daisy is a sweet and playful name.

14. Ember: an English name that means "spark". It is a nature name that means "warmth and light." Ember is a distinct and vivacious name.

15. Fern: a name that means "fern plant" in English. It is a botanical name associated with growth and nature. Fern is a straightforward and elegant name.

16. Flora: is a Latin name that means "flower". It became popular as a result of the Roman goddess of flowers. Flora is a botanical name that means "beauty and nature."

17. Gaia: is a Greek name that means "earth." It became popular because of the Greek goddess of the earth. Gaia is a powerful and inspiring name.

18. Hazel: a name that means "hazel tree" in English. It is a nature name that means "wisdom and protection." Hazel is a timeless and classic name.

19. Iris: is a Greek name that means "rainbow". It became popular because of the Greek goddess of the rainbow. Iris is a beautiful and mystical name.

20. Ivy: is an English name that means "ivy plant." It is a botanical name associated with growth and nature. Ivy is a straightforward and elegant name.

21. Jade: is a Spanish name that means "side stone." It is a name for a gemstone associated with beauty and strength. Jade is a distinctive and exotic name.

22. Jasmine: is a Persian name that means "God's gift." It became popular because of the fragrant flower jasmine. Jasmine is a lovely and elegant name.

23. Juniper: a Latin name that means "juniper tree" It is a natural name that means "protection and healing." Juniper is a distinctive and natural name.

24. Lark: an English name that means "songbird" It is a nature name that means "freedom and joy." Lark is a sweet and playful name.

25. Laurel is a Latin name that means "laurel tree." It is a nature name associated with victory and accomplishment. Laurel is a timeless and classic name.

26. Lily: is a Latin name that means "lily flower." It is a botanical name associated with innocence and purity. Lily is a timeless and classic name.

27. Luna: is a Latin name that means "moon". It became popular because of the Roman goddess of the moon. The name Luna is associated with the night sky and is mystical and enchanting.

28. Lyra: is a Greek name that means "lyre". It gained popularity because of the constellation Lyra, which is associated with Orpheus' lyre. Lyra is a memorable and musical name.

29. Magnolia: is a Latin name that means "magnolia tree." It is a botanical name that connotes beauty and grace. Magnolia is a lovely and elegant name.

30. Maple: an English name that means "maple tree". It is a nature name associated with endurance and strength. Maple is a distinctive and natural name.

31. Marigold: a name that means "golden flower" in English. It is a botanical name that connotes warmth and happiness. Marigold is a sweet and playful name.

32. Meadow: is an English name that means "meadow". It is a nature name associated with serenity and peace. Meadow is a straightforward and elegant name.

33. Ocean: is a name that means "ocean" in English. It is a nature name that connotes vastness and depth. Ocean is a one-of-a-kind and natural name.

34. Olive: a name that means "olive tree" in English. It is a nature name that means "peace and wisdom." Olive is a timeless and classic name.

35. Pearl: is a name that means "pearl" in English. It is a gemstone name that connotes beauty and purity. Pearl is a timeless and classic name.

36. Phoenix: is a Greek name that means "dark red". It became popular as a result of the mythical bird that rises from the ashes. Phoenix is a powerful and inspiring name.

37. Poppy: a name that means "poppy flower" in English. It is a botanical name associated with beauty and memory. Poppy is a sweet and playful name.

38. Primrose: a name that means "first rose" in English. It is a botanical name that represents beauty and new beginnings. Primrose is a sweet and playful name.

39. Robin: is an English name that means "bright fame." It is a nature name that means "joy and happiness." Robin is a timeless and classic name.

40. Rose: a Latin name that means "rose flower" It's a botanical name that means "beauty and love." Rose is a timeless and classic name.

41. Ruby: a Latin name that means "red gemstone". It is a gemstone name associated with vigor and passion. Ruby is a powerful and inspiring name.

42. Sage: is a name that means "wise one" in English. It's a nature name that means "wisdom and healing." Sage is a one-of-a-kind and natural name.

43. Sapphire: is a Greek name that means "blue gemstone". It is a gemstone name that represents wisdom and truth. Sapphire is a beautiful and mystical name.

44. Savannah: is an English name that means "treeless plain." It is a nature name that connotes openness and freedom. Savannah is a one-of-a-kind and natural name.

45. Sierra: a Spanish name that means "mountain range" It is a nature name associated with endurance and strength. Sierra is a one-of-a-kind and natural name.

46. Skye: a Scottish name that means "sky" It is a nature name associated with openness and freedom. Skye is a one-of-a-kind and natural name.

47. Sparrow: is an English name that means "sparrow bird." It is a nature name that means "freedom and joy." Sparrow is a sweet and playful name.

48. Starling: means "starling bird" in English. It is a nature name that means "freedom and joy." Starling is a one-of-a-kind and natural name.

49. Violet: is a name that means "violet flower" in English. It is a botanical name that connotes beauty and innocence. Violet is a timeless and classic name.

50. Willow: is a name that means "willow tree" in English. It is a natural name associated with adaptability and resilience. Willow is a one-of-a-kind and natural name.

51. Wren: is an English name that means "wren bird." It is a nature name that means "freedom and joy." Wren is a sweet and playful name.

52. Zinnia: a Latin name that means "zinnia flower." It is a botanical name associated with beauty and individuality. Zinnia is a one-of-a-kind and natural name.

Color Names

1. Amber: Inspired by the golden color of amber, this name means "jewel."

2. Aquamarine: This name is derived from the gemstone's blue-green color and means "seawater."

3. Auburn: This name is derived from the color reddish-brown and means "reddish-brown".

4. Azure: This name is inspired by the sky's blue color and means "sky-blue."

5. Beige: Inspired by the light brown color, this name is both unique and modern.

6. Bianca: This name is inspired by the color white and means "white".

7. Blue: Inspired by the color blue, this name is both unique and modern.

8. Burgundy: Inspired by the deep red color, this name is both unique and modern.

9. Berry is a unisex name that is derived from the old English word "Bernie," which means berry.

10. Cerulean: Inspired by the blue-green color of the sky, this name means "heavenly blue."

11. Cinnamon: Inspired by the brownish-red color of cinnamon spice, this name means "spice."

12. Clover: Inspired by the green color and shape of clover leaves, this name means "clover."

13. Cocoa: Inspired by the brown color of cocoa beans, this name means "chocolate."

14. Copper: Inspired by the reddish-brown color of copper metal, this name means "copper."

15. Coral: Inspired by the pink-orange color of coral, this name means "coral."

16. Coralie: This name is derived from the pink-orange color of coral and means "coral".

17. Cream: Inspired by the light yellow color, this name is both unique and modern.

18. Crimson: Inspired by the deep red color, this name means "crimson".

19. Carmine: This name is derived from the deep red color and means "crimson".

20. Daisy: means "day's eye" and is inspired by the white and yellow color of daisies.

21. Ebony: Inspired by the black color of ebony wood, this name means "dark beauty."

22. Emerald: Inspired by the green color of emerald gemstones, this name means "precious gem."

23. Flora: Inspired by the colors of flowers, this name means "flower."

24. Fuchsia: Inspired by the vibrant pink color, this name is a unique and daring choice.

25. Garnet: This name is derived from the deep red color of the gemstone and means "garnet".

26. Ginger: This name is derived from the reddish-brown color of ginger root and means "ginger-haired".

27. Gingerbread: Inspired by the brown color and sweet scent of gingerbread, this name is a unique and modern choice.

28. Goldie: This name is derived from the color gold and means "golden".

29. Hazel: Inspired by the brownish-green color of hazelnuts, this name means "hazel tree."

30. Hazelwood: Inspired by the brownish-green color of hazelnuts, this name means "hazel tree."

31. Honey: Inspired by the golden color of honey, this name means "sweet as honey."

33. Indigo: Inspired by the rich, deep blue color, this name means "Indian dye."

33. Ivory: This name is inspired by the white color and smooth texture of ivory and means "ivory".

34. Jade: Inspired by the green color of jade gemstones, this name means "precious stone."

35. Jadeite: Inspired by the green color of jadeite gemstones, this name means "precious stone."

36. Jasmine: Inspired by the white color and sweet scent of jasmine flowers, this name means "gift from God."

37. Kelly: Inspired by the bright green color, this name means "warrior."

38. Khaki: Inspired by the beige-green color, this name is both unique and modern.

39. Lavender: This name, which means "lavender flower," is inspired by the purple color and sweet scent of lavender flowers.

40. Lilac: Inspired by the pale purple color of lilac flowers, this name means "pale purple."

41. Lilith: Inspired by the pale purple color of lilacs, this name means "ghost" or "night monster."

42. Mahogany: Inspired by the reddish-brown color of mahogany wood, this name is both unique and modern.

43. Maple: Inspired by the reddish-brown color of maple leaves in the fall, this name means "maple tree."

44. Marigold: Inspired by the bright orange-yellow color of marigold flowers, this name means "golden flower."

45. Mauve: Inspired by the pale purple-pink color, this name is both unique and modern.

46. Midnight: Inspired by the dark blue color of midnight, this name is both unique and modern.

47. Mocha: Inspired by the brown color and sweet taste of mocha coffee, this name means "coffee."

48. Moss: Inspired by the green color and texture of moss, this name means "moss".

49. Navy: Inspired by the dark blue color, this name is both unique and modern.

50. Navya: is a name inspired by the color navy blue and means "new."

51. Nevaeh: This unique and modern name is inspired by the word "heaven" spelled backward.

52. Noir: This name is inspired by the color black and means "dark".

53. Olive: Inspired by the greenish-brown color of olives, this name means "olive tree."

54. Olivia: Inspired by the color olive green, this name means "olive tree."

55. Onyx: Inspired by the black color of onyx gemstones, this name means "claw" or "fingernail."

56. Peach: This name is inspired by the pink-orange color of peaches and means "peach".

57. Pearl: This name is inspired by the white color and smooth texture of pearls and means "pearl".

58. Quartz: Inspired by the clear color of quartz gemstones, this name is a unique and modern choice.

59. Raven: Inspired by the black color of ravens, this name means "blackbird."

60. Rose: This name is inspired by the pink and red colors of roses and means "rose".

61. Saffron: Inspired by the yellow-orange color of saffron spice, this name means "yellow spice."

62. Sage: Inspired by the grayish-green color of sage leaves, this name means "wise".

63. Tangerine: This name was inspired by the orange color of tangerines and means "orange-red".

64. Teal: Inspired by the blue-green color of teal, this name is unique and modern.

65. Umber: Inspired by the brown color of raw umber pigment, this name is both unique and modern.

66. Violet: Inspired by the purple color of violets, this name means "violet flower."

67. Willow: Inspired by the green color and graceful branches of willow trees, this name means "willow tree."

68. Xanthe: This name was inspired by the color yellow and means "yellow".

69. Yarrow: Inspired by the yellow color of yarrow flowers, this name means "healing herb."

70. Zinnia: Inspired by the vibrant colors of zinnia flowers, this name means "zinnia flower."

Place Names

1. Adelaide: This name means "noble kind" and is derived from Adelaide, Australia.

2. Alexandria: The name Alexandria means "defender of the people" and is derived from the Egyptian city of Alexandria.

3. Amara: The name Amara means "eternal" and is derived from the Nigerian city of Amara.

4. Annapurna: The name Annapurna means "goddess of food" and is derived from the Nepalese mountain range.

5. Aspen: This name means "tree" and was inspired by the town of Aspen, Colorado.

6. Athens: This name means "wise" and is derived from the Greek city-state of Athens.

7. Atlanta: This name means "strong" and was inspired by Atlanta, Georgia.

8. Aurora: This name means "dawn" and is derived from Aurora, Illinois.

9. Austin: This name means "great" and was inspired by Austin, Texas.

10. Bali: The name Bali means "offerings" and is derived from the Indonesian island of Bali.

11. Berlin: This name means "swamp" and was inspired by Germany's capital city.

12. Beverly: This name means "from the beaver meadow" and was inspired by the city of Beverly in Massachusetts.

13. Brooklyn: This name means "brook" and is derived from the borough of Brooklyn in New York City.

14. Calais: This name means "beautiful" and is derived from the French city of Calais.

15. Camden: This name means "winding valley" and was inspired by the city of Camden, New Jersey.

16. Capri: This name means "goat" in Italian and is derived from the Italian island of Capri.

17. Carmel: This name translates to "vineyard" and is based on the California town of Carmel.

18. Carolina: This name means "free person" and is derived from the state of North Carolina in the United States.

19. Catalina: This name means "pure" and is derived from Catalina Island in California.

20. Charlotte: This name means "free woman" and was inspired by the city of Charlotte, North Carolina.

21. Chelsea: This name means "landing place" and is derived from the Chelsea neighborhood of London.

22. Cheyenne: This name means "people of a different speech" and is derived from the Wyoming city of Cheyenne.

23. Chicago: This name means "wild onion" and was inspired by the city of Chicago, Illinois.

24. China: This name means "middle kingdom" and is derived from the Chinese country.

25. Dakota is a name that means "friend" and is derived from the US states of North and South Dakota.

26. Dallas: The name Dallas means "skilled" and is derived from the Texas city of Dallas.

27. Delhi: The name Delhi means "hill" and is derived from the Indian city of Delhi.

28. Denver: This name means "green valley" and was inspired by Denver, Colorado.

29. Devon: This name means "defender" and is derived from the English county of Devon.

30. Dublin: This name means "black pool" and was inspired by Ireland's capital city.

31. Eden: This name translates as "delightful place" and is based on the biblical Garden of Eden.

32. Egypt: This name means "temple of the soul" and is derived from the Egyptian country.

33. Elba: This name means "swan" and is derived from the Italian island of Elba.

34. Florence: The name Florence means "prosperous" and is derived from the Italian city of Florence.

35. Georgia: This name means "farmer" and was inspired by the state of Georgia in the United States.

36. Glasgow: This name translates as "dear green place" and is based on the Scottish city of Glasgow.

37. Harlem: This name means "home" and was inspired by the Harlem neighborhood of New York City.

38. Havana: This name means "habitation" and is derived from the Cuban capital of Havana.

39. Helena: This name means "bright" and was inspired by Helena, Montana.

40. Holland: This name means "wooded land" and is derived from the Dutch country.

41. Houston: This name means "hill" and was inspired by Houston, Texas.

42. India: This name means "river" and was inspired by the Indian country.

43. Indiana: This name means "land of the Indians" and is derived from the state of Indiana in the United States.

44. Ireland: This name means "green" and was inspired by Ireland.

45. Israel: The name Israel means "wrestles with God" and is derived from the country of Israel.

46. Jamaica: This name translates as "land of wood and water" and is derived from the Caribbean island of Jamaica.

47. Jersey: The name Jersey means "island of the hawks" and is derived from the Channel Island of Jersey.

48. Jordan: This name means "descend" and is derived from the Jordan River and country.

49. Kenya: This name means "mountain" and is derived from Kenya, an African country.

50. Kingston: This name means "king's town" and is derived from Kingston, Jamaica's capital city.

51. Kyoto: This name translates to "capital city" and is based on the Japanese city of Kyoto.

52. Laredo: The name Laredo means "golden" and is derived from the Texas city of Laredo.

53 Lhasa: This name means "place of the gods" and is derived from the Tibetan city of Lhasa.

54. London: This name means "fortress of the moon" and is based on England's capital city.

55. Louisiana: This name translates as "Land of Louis" and is based on the US state of Louisiana.

56. Madison: This name means "son of Maud" and was inspired by the city of Madison, Wisconsin.

57. Malibu: This name means "place of the surf" and is derived from the California town of Malibu.

58. Manila: This name means "place of the nila plant" and is derived from the Philippines' capital city.

59. Marbella: This name means "beautiful sea" and is derived from the Spanish town of Marbella.

60. Memphis: This name means "enduring and beautiful" and was inspired by the city of Memphis, Tennessee.

61. Miami: This name means "sweet water" and was inspired by the city of Miami in Florida.

62. Milan: The name Milan means "lover of grace" and is derived from the Italian city of Milan.

63. Monaco: This name means "solitary" and is derived from the principality of Monaco.

64. Montana: This name means "mountainous" and is derived from the state of Montana in the United States.

65. Montreal: This name translates as "royal mountain" and is based on the Canadian city of Montreal.

66. Moscow: This name means "swampy place" and is based on Russia's capital city.

Nairobi: This name means "cool waters" and was inspired by Nairobi, Kenya's capital city.

68. Nashville: This name means "city of music" and was inspired by Nashville, Tennessee.

69. Nevada: This name means "snowy" and is derived from the state of Nevada in the United States.

70. New Orleans: This name means "new city" and was inspired by the city of New Orleans in Louisiana.

71. Nova: The name Nova means "new" and is derived from the Canadian province of Nova Scotia.

72. Odesa: The name Odesa means "long journey" and is derived from the Ukrainian city of Odesa.

73. Olympia: The name Olympia means "mountain of the gods" and is derived from the Greek city of Olympia.

74. Orlando: This name means "famous throughout the land" and is based on the city of Orlando, Florida.

75. Osaka: This name means "big hill" in Japanese and is based on the Japanese city of Osaka.

76. Oslo: This name means "God's Field" and was inspired by Norway's capital city.

77. Paris: This name means "from Paris" and was inspired by France's capital city.

78. Phoenix: This name means "mythical bird" and was inspired by the city of Phoenix, Arizona.

79. Prague: This name means "threshold" and was inspired by the Czech Republic's capital city.

80. Quebec: This name translates as "where the river narrows" and is derived from the Canadian province of Quebec.

81. Raleigh: This name means "meadow of deer" and was inspired by Raleigh, North Carolina.

82. Rio: This name means "river" and is derived from Rio de Janeiro, Brazil.

83. Rome: This name means "from Rome" and was inspired by Italy's capital city.

84. Salem: This name means "peaceful" and was inspired by the city of Salem, Massachusetts.

85. San Diego: This name means "Saint James" and was inspired by the city of San Diego in California.

86. Santa Fe: This name means "holy faith" and was inspired by the city of Santa Fe in New Mexico.

86. Savannah: This name means "flat land" and was inspired by Savannah, Georgia.

88. Seattle: This name means "dweller by the sea" and was inspired by the Washington city of Seattle.

89. Sedona: This name means "from Sedona" and is derived from the Arizona town of the same name.

90. Sevilla: The name Sevilla means "youthful" and is derived from the Spanish city of Seville.

91. Shanghai: The name Shanghai means "above the sea" and is derived from the Chinese city of Shanghai.

92. Sicily: The name Sicily means "from Sicily" and is derived from the Italian island of Sicily.

93. Sydney: This name means "wide island" and was inspired by Sydney, Australia.

94. Tahoe: This name means "edge of the lake" and is derived from Lake Tahoe in

California and Nevada.

95. Tennessee: This name means "bend in the river" and is derived from the state of Tennessee in the United States.

96. Texas: This name means "friends" and is derived from the state of Texas in the United States.

97. Tokyo: This name means "eastern capital" and is based on Japan's capital city.

98. Toronto: The name Toronto means "meeting place" and is derived from the Canadian city of Toronto.

99. Valencia: The name Valencia means "brave" and is derived from the Spanish city of Valencia.

100. Venice: This name means "from Venice" and is based on the Italian city.

101. Vermont: This name means "green mountain" and is derived from the state of Vermont in the United States.

102. Vienna: This name means "white" and was inspired by Austria's capital city.

103. Virginia: This name means "pure" and is derived from the state of Virginia in the United States.

104. Wales: This name means "from Wales" and was inspired by the Welsh country.

105. Washington: This name means "estate of a wealthy person" and is derived from the state of Washington in the United States.

106. Wellington: This name means "wealthy estate" and was inspired by New Zealand's capital city.

107. West: This name means "from the west" and is derived from the direction.

108. Wyoming: This name means "large plains" and is derived from the US state of Wyoming.

109. Zurich: The name Zurich means "water" and is derived from the Swiss city of Zurich.

Nicknames

1. Aggie: is a diminutive of the Greek names Agnes and Agatha, which mean "chaste" and "good," respectively. Aggie is a sweet and lively name.

2. Agnes: a Greek name that means "chaste". It rose to prominence as a result of Saint Agnes, a Christian martyr. Agnes is a timeless and classic name.

3. Allie: an English name that means "noble". It is a short form of the names Alice or Alison. Allie is a sweet and lively name.

4. Ally: an English name that means "noble". It is a short form of the names Alice or Alison. Ally is a sweet and lively name.

5. Alma: Alma is a Latin name that means "nurturing" or "kind." It is a name that evokes feelings of warmth and compassion.

6. Amy: is a name that means "beloved" in English. It's a name that connotes sweetness and kindness. Amy is a timeless and classic name.

7. Annie: is a name that means "grace" in English. It is a short form of the names Ann or Anna. Annie is a sweet and lively name.

8. Ara: is an Armenian name that means "brings rain". It is a name associated with growth and fertility. Ara is a one-of-a-kind and exotic name.

9. Ari: is a Hebrew name that means "lion". It is a name associated with bravery and strength. Ari is a powerful and inspiring name.

10. Bea: is a Latin name that means "blessed". It is a short form of the name Beatrice. Bea is a charming and spunky name.

11. Bella: is an Italian name that means "beautiful". It rose to prominence as a result of the character Bella Swan in the "Twilight" series. Bella is a lovely and elegant name.

12. Belle: is a French name that means "beautiful." It rose to prominence as a result of the character Belle in the fairy tale "Beauty and the Beast." Belle is a lovely and elegant name.

13. Bess: an English name that means "God is my oath." It is a short form of the name Elizabeth. Bess is a sweet and lively name.

14. Bessie: an English name that means "God is my oath." It is a short form of the name Elizabeth. Bessie is a sweet and lively name.

15. Beth is a Hebrew name that means "God's house." It is a short form of the name Elizabeth. Beth is a straightforward and elegant name.

16. Betty is an English name that means "God is my oath." It is a short form of the name Elizabeth. Betty is a timeless and classic name.

17. Birdie is an English name that means "little bird." It is a name associated with liberty and joy. Birdie is a sweet and playful name.

18. Cami is an English name that means "priest's helper." Camilla is a diminutive of the name. Cami is a sweet and lively name.

19. Cammy is an English name that means "priest's helper." Camilla is a diminutive of the name. Cammy is a sweet and lively name.

20. Cece is an English name that means "blind". It is a short form of the name Cecilia. Cece is a sweet and lively name.

21. Celia is a Latin name that means "heavenly". It is a name associated with grace and beauty. Celia is a lovely name that is both simple and elegant.

22. Cleo is a Greek name that means "glory". Cleopatra, the Egyptian queen, popularized it. Cleo is a one-of-a-kind and exotic name.

23. Coco is a French name that means "help". It is a name associated with power and independence. Coco is a distinct and endearing name.

24. Cora is a Greek name that means "maiden". It is a name associated with innocence and purity. Cora is a straightforward and elegant name.

25. Cori is a Greek name that means "maiden". It is a name associated with innocence and purity. Cori is a sweet and lively name.

26. Della is an English name that means "noble". It is a name associated with grace and elegance. Della is a straightforward and elegant name.

27. Didi is a Hebrew name that means "beloved". It's a name that connotes sweetness and kindness. Didi is a distinct and vivacious name.

28. Dottie is an English name that means "God's gift." It is a short form of the name Dorothy. Dottie is a sweet and lively name.

29. Edie: an English name that means "prosperous in war." It is a short form of the name Edith. Edie is a sweet and lively name.

30. Effie is a Greek name that means "well-spoken." It is a name synonymous with intelligence and eloquence. Effie is a distinct and vivacious name.

31. Elsie is a Scottish name that means "pledged to God." It is a short form of the name Elizabeth. Elsie is a sweet and lively name.

32. Emmy is a name that means "universal" in English. It is a short form of the names Emily or Emma. Emmy is a sweet and lively name.

33. Essie: an English name that means "star" It is a short form of the name Esther.

Essie is a sweet and lively name.

34. Evie is a Hebrew name that means "life" or "living one." It is a short form of the name Eve or Evelyn. Evie is a sweet and lively name.

35. Fifi is a French name that means "Jehovah grows." It is a short form of the name Josephine. Fifi is a sweet and lively name.

36. Frankie: an English name that means "free one" It is a short form of the names Frances or Francis. Frankie is a charming and endearing name.

37. Gigi is a French name that means "earth worker." It is a short form of the names Georgina or Virginia. Gigi is a sweet and lively name.

38. Goldie: an English name that means "made of gold." It is a name associated with wealth and success. Goldie is a distinct and endearing name.

39. Gracie: an English name that means "grace". It is a short form of the name Grace. Gracie is a sweet and lively name.

40. Hattie is an English name that means "home-ruler." It is a short form of the name Harriet. Hattie is a sweet and lively name.

41. Hazel: a name that means "hazel tree" in English. It is a name associated with knowledge and protection. Hazel is a lovely name that is both simple and elegant.

42. Izzy is a Hebrew name that means "God is my oath." It is a short form of the names Isabel or Isabella. Izzy is a sweet and lively name.

43. Jo: an English name that means "God is gracious". It is a short form of the names Joanna or Josephine. Jo is a straightforward and elegant name.

44. Josie: an English name that means "God will increase". It is a short form of the name Josephine. Josie is a sweet and lively name.

45. Joy: is an English name that means "happiness." It is a name associated with happiness and positivity. Joy is a straightforward and elegant name.

46. Junie: is a Latin name that means "young". It is a short form of the names Junia or Juniper. Junie is a sweet and lively name.

47. Kiki: a French name that means "double happiness." It is a short form of the names Kiana or Kiara. Kiki is a sweet and lively name.

48. Kitty: is an English name that means "pure". It's a diminutive of Katherine or Kathleen. Kitty is a sweet and lively name.

49. Lainey: an English name that means "bright light" It is a short form of the names Elaine or Lorraine. Lainey is a sweet and lively name.

50. Lark: is an English name that means "songbird." It is a name associated with liberty and joy. Lark is a whimsical and unusual name.

51. Lea: is a Hebrew name that means "weary." It is a name associated with fortitude and perseverance. The name Lea is both simple and elegant.

52. Libby: is an English name that means "pledged to God." It is a short form of the name Elizabeth. Libby is a sweet and lively name.

53. Lila: is a Sanskrit name that means "playful." It is a name associated with imagination and creativity. Lila is a lovely name that is both simple and elegant.

54. Lili: is a Hebrew name that means "My God is my oath." It is a short form of the name Elizabeth. Lili is a sweet and lively name.

55. Lina: a Latin name that means "palm tree" It is a name associated with tranquillity and peace. Lina is a straightforward and elegant name.

56. Liv: is a Scandinavian name that means "life". It's a name that connotes vitality and energy. Liv is a straightforward and elegant name.

57. Lottie: an English name that means "free man" It is a short form of the name Charlotte. Lottie is a sweet and lively name.

58. Lou: is a French name that means "famous warrior." It is a short form of the names Louise or Louisa. Lou is a straightforward and elegant name.

59. Lucy: an English name that means "light" It's a name that connotes intelligence and clarity. Lucy is a timeless and classic name.

60. Lulu: is an Arabic name that means "pearl". It's a name synonymous with beauty and elegance. Lulu is a sweet and lively name.

61. Mabel: is an English name that means "lovable." It's a name that connotes sweetness and kindness. Mabel is a timeless and classic name.

62. Maisie: is a Scottish name that means "pearl". It is a short form of the name Margaret. Maisie is a sweet and lively name.

63. Mamie: is an English name that means "pearl". It is a short form of the name Margaret. Mamie is a sweet and lively name.

64. Millie: is an English name that means "gentle strength." It's a diminutive of Millicent or Mildred. Millie is a sweet and lively name.

65. Minnie: is an English name that means "God's will." It is a short form of the names Minerva or Wilhelmina. Minnie is a sweet and lively name.

66. Mira: is a Latin name that means "wonderful" or "admirable." It is also derived from the Sanskrit word for "sea" or "ocean". Mira is a lovely and elegant name.

67. Molly: is an English name derived from Mary that means "bitter" or "beloved." It's a classic and timeless name.

68. Nell: a diminutive of Helen or Eleanor that means "bright" or "shining one." It's a straightforward and timeless name.

69. Nellie: is a diminutive of Helen or Eleanor that means "bright" or "shining one." It's adorable and vintage.

69. Nellie: is a diminutive of Helen or Eleanor that means "bright" or "shining one." It's a sweet and retro name.

70. Nessa: is a Hebrew name that means "miracle" or "sign". It's a one-of-a-kind and enigmatic name.

71. Nia: is a Welsh name that means "bright" or "radiant". It's a short and simple name.

72. Nicky: is a nickname for Nicole or Nicholas that means "people's victory." It's a gender-neutral name that can be used for both boys and girls.

72. Nola: is an Irish name that means "famous" or "noble". It's a fun and lively name.

74. Nona: is a Latin name that means "ninth" in English. It's a one-of-a-kind and uncommon name.

75. Nora: is an Irish name that means "honor" or "light." It is a timeless and classic name.

76. Olive: is an English name that means "olive tree." It represents both peace and abundance. Olive is a name that is both vintage and nature-inspired.

77. Ollie: is a nickname for Oliver or Olivia that means "olive tree." It's a cute and fun name.

78. Patsy: is a diminutive of Patricia, which means "noble" or "patrician." It's a charming and vintage name.

79. Penny: is a Greek name that means "weaver" or "bobbin worker." It's a cute and upbeat name.

80. Perry: a name of English origin that means "pear tree" It's a gender-neutral name that can be used for both boys and girls.

81. Poppy: is a Latin name that refers to the flower of the same name. It is a symbol of beauty and remembrance. Poppy is a bright and playful name.

82. Posy: is an English name that means "small bouquet". It's a lovely and delicate name.

83. Rae: is a Hebrew name that means "ewe" or "female sheep". It's a short and powerful name.

84. Rainy: is a name derived from the word "rain" in English. It's a one-of-a-kind

kind name inspired by nature.

85. Reggie: is a nickname for Reginald that means "counsel power." It's a lively and playful name.

86. Remy: is a French name that means "oarsman" or "remedy." It's a gender-neutral name that can be used for both boys and girls.

87. Rosie: is a diminutive of the name Rose, referring to the same-named flower. It's a lovely and romantic name.

88. Ruby: is an English name that refers to the gemstone of the same name. It represents love and passion. Ruby is a timeless and sophisticated name.

89. Sadie: is a Hebrew name that means "princess." It's a charming and vintage name.

90. Sally: is a diminutive of Sarah which means "princess." It's a welcoming and approachable name.

91. Sam: is a unisex Hebrew name that means "heard by God." It's a short and powerful name.

92. Sammy: a diminutive of Samuel or Samantha that means "heard by God." It's a fun and friendly name.

93. Sandy: is a diminutive of Sandra or Alexander which means "defender of mankind." It's a gender-neutral name that can be used for both boys and girls.

94. Scout: is an English name that means "to listen" or "to observe". It's a unique and daring name.

95. Stevie: is a nickname for Stephanie or Steven that means "crown" or "garland." It's a gender-neutral name that can be used for both boys and girls.

96. Sunny: is a name derived from the English word "sun". It's a happy and bright name.

97. Susie: is a diminutive of the names Susan or Susanna, which means "lily" or "rose." It's a sweet and welcoming name.

98. Sylvie: is a French name that means "from the forest." It's a lovely, nature-inspired name.

99. Tessa: is a diminutive of the names Theresa or Esther, meaning "harvester" or "star". It's a lovely, sophisticated name.

100. Tillie: is a diminutive of Matilda, which means "strength in battle." It's a charming and vintage name.

101. Trixie: a diminutive of Beatrix or Patricia, meaning "voyager" or "noble." It's a lively and playful name.

102. Vee: is a short form of names beginning with the letter V, such as Veronica or Victoria. It's a fun and short name.

103. Vivi: is a diminutive of names beginning with the letter V, such as Vivian or Victoria. It's fun alongside an upbeat name.

104. Winnie: is a diminutive of Winifred or Edwina which means "holy reconciliation" or "friend of wealth."

Middle Names

1. Ada: is a Germanic name meaning "noble" or "nobility". It is a classic and timeless name that has been popular for centuries.

2. Adaline: is a Germanic name meaning "noble kind". It is a variant of the name Adeline and has a classic and elegant sound to it.

3. Adele: is a Germanic name meaning "noble" or "kind". It gained popularity due to the singer Adele. Adele is a classic and elegant name.

4. Alice: is a Germanic name meaning "noble" or "of noble birth". It gained popularity due to the character Alice in Lewis Carroll's "Alice's Adventures in Wonderland." Alice is a classic and timeless name

5. Amelia-Rose: Amelia is a Germanic name meaning "work" or "industrious". Rose is a Latin name meaning "rose flower". Amelia-Rose is a beautiful and feminine name that combines two classic names

6. Amy-Leigh: Amy is a French name meaning "beloved". Leigh is an English name meaning "meadow". Amy-Leigh is a cute and spunky name that combines two classic names.

7. Ana: is a Spanish name meaning "gracious" or "full of grace". It is a variant of the name Anna and has a simple and elegant sound to it.

8. Angelique: is a French name meaning "angelic" or "like an angel". It is a variant of the name Angelica and has a sophisticated and elegant sound to it.

9. Arleth: is a Spanish name meaning "pledge" or "oath". It is a unique and exotic name that is associated with loyalty and commitment.

10. Artemis: is a Greek name meaning "goddess of the hunt". It gained popularity due to the character Artemis Fowl in Eoin Colfer's novel series. Artemis is a strong and empowering name.

11. Athena: is a Greek name meaning "goddess of wisdom and war". It gained popularity due to the character Athena in Greek mythology. Athena is a strong and intelligent name.

12. Aubrey: is a French name meaning "elf ruler". It gained popularity due to the character Aubrey in the movie "The Breakfast Club." Aubrey is a cute and spunky name.

13. Belle: is a French name meaning "beautiful". It gained popularity due to the character Belle in Disney's "Beauty and the Beast." Belle is a classic and elegant name.

14. Blaire: is a Scottish name meaning "dweller on the plain". It is a unisex name that has a strong and empowering sound to it.

15. Dakota: is a Native American name meaning "friend" or "ally". It gained popularity due to the actress Dakota Fanning. Dakota is a unique and exotic name.

16. Eden: is a Hebrew name meaning "delight" or "paradise". It gained popularity due to the biblical Garden of Eden. Eden is a beautiful and serene name.

17. Emberlynn: is a combination of the names Ember and Lynn. Ember is an English name meaning "spark" or "burning low". Lynn is a Welsh name meaning "lake". Emberlynn is a unique and whimsical name.

18. Eve: is a Hebrew name meaning "life" or "living one". It gained popularity due to the biblical character Eve. Eve is a classic and timeless name.

19. Flora: is a Latin name meaning "flower". It gained popularity due to the Roman goddess of flowers and spring. Flora is a timeless and elegant name.

20. Freya: is a Norse name meaning "lady" or "mistress". It gained popularity due to the Norse goddess of love and fertility. Freya is a strong and empowering name.

21. Gaia: is a Greek name meaning "earth mother". It gained popularity due to the Greek goddess of the earth. Gaia is a unique and mystical name.

22. Gia: is an Italian name meaning "God is gracious". It gained popularity due to the model Gia Carangi. Gia is a simple and elegant name.

23. Hermione: is a Greek name meaning "messenger" or "earthly". It gained popularity due to the character Hermione Granger in J.K. Rowling's "Harry Potter" series. Hermione is a strong and intelligent name.

24. Ida: is a Germanic name meaning "hardworking" or "industrious". It is a classic and timeless name that has been popular for centuries.

25. Ivy: is an English name meaning "ivy plant". It is a botanical name that is associated with nature and beauty. Ivy is a simple and elegant name.

26. Jane: is an English name meaning "God is gracious". It gained popularity due to the character Jane Eyre in Charlotte Bronte's novel. Jane is a classic and timeless name.

27. Jaya: is a Sanskrit name meaning "victory". It is a unique and exotic name that is associated with strength and success.

28. Juno: is a Latin name meaning "queen of the heavens". It gained popularity due to the Roman goddess of marriage and childbirth. Juno is a strong and empowering name.

29. Kali: is a Sanskrit name meaning "black" or "time". It gained popularity due to the Hindu goddess of destruction and transformation.

30. Kay: is a Welsh name meaning "rejoice". It gained popularity due to the character Kay in Arthurian legend. Kay is a simple and elegant name.

31. Kit: is a diminutive of the name Christopher, meaning "bearer of Christ". It gained popularity due to the character Kit Tyler in Elizabeth George Speare's novel "The Witch of Blackbird Pond." Kit is a cute and spunky name.

32. Lia: is a Hebrew name meaning "weary" or "tired". It is a variant of the name Leah and has a simple and elegant sound to it.

33. Luna: is a Latin name meaning "moon". It gained popularity due to the Roman goddess of the moon. Luna is a mystical and enchanting name.

34. Mia: is a Scandinavian name meaning "mine" or "beloved". It gained popularity due to the actress Mia Farrow. Mia is a cute and spunky name.

35. Minerva: is a Latin name meaning "goddess of wisdom". It gained popularity due to the Roman goddess of wisdom. Minerva is a strong and intelligent name.

36. Murphy: is an Irish name meaning "sea warrior". It is a unisex name that has a strong and empowering sound to it

37. Noelle: is a French name meaning "Christmas". It is a variant of the name Noel and has a festive and cheerful sound to it.

38. Ophelia: is a Greek name meaning "help" or "aid". It gained popularity due to the character Ophelia in Shakespeare's play "Hamlet." Ophelia is a romantic and tragic name.

39. Padma: is a Sanskrit name meaning "lotus". It gained popularity due to the Hindu goddess of wealth and prosperity. Padma is a unique and exotic name.

40. Parker: is an English name meaning "park keeper". It is a unisex name that has a strong and empowering sound to it.

41. Persephone: is a Greek name meaning "bringer of destruction". It gained popularity due to the Greek goddess of the underworld. Persephone is a strong and empowering name.

42. Phoebe: is a Greek name meaning "bright" or "pure". It gained popularity due to the character Phoebe Buffay in the TV show "Friends." Phoebe is a cute and spunky name.

43. Raya: is a Hebrew name meaning "friend". It is a unique and exotic name that is associated with loyalty and friendship.

44. Reese: is a Welsh name meaning "enthusiasm". It gained popularity due to the actress Reese Witherspoon. Reese is a cute and spunky name.

45. Remi: is a French name meaning "oarsman". It is a unisex name that has a strong and empowering sound to it.

46. River: is an English name meaning "stream of water". It gained popularity due to the actor River Phoenix. River is a unique and natural name.

47. Rose: is a Latin name meaning "rose flower". It is a botanical name that is associated with beauty and love. Rose is a classic and timeless name.

48. Rowan: is a Gaelic name meaning "little red one". It is a unisex name that has a strong and empowering sound to it.

49. Rylee: is an Irish name meaning "courageous". It is a variant of the name Riley and has a strong and empowering sound to it.

50. Thora: is a Scandinavian name meaning "thunder". It gained popularity due to the character Thora Birch in the movie "American Beauty." Thora is a strong and empowering name.

51. Uma: is a Sanskrit name meaning "tranquility". It gained popularity due to the actress Uma Thurman. Uma is a unique and exotic name.

52. Vida: is a Spanish name meaning "life". It is a simple and elegant name that is associated with vitality and energy.

53. Wrenley: is a combination of the names Wren and Leigh. Wren is an English name meaning "small bird". Leigh is an English name meaning "meadow". Wrenley is a unique and whimsical name.

54. Ziva: is a Hebrew name meaning "radiance" or "brightness". It gained popularity due to the character Ziva David in the TV show "NCIS." Ziva is a unique and exotic name.

Unisex Names

1. Addison: an English name that means "son of Adam" It is a name connected with fortitude and perseverance.

2. Alex is a Greek name that means "people's defender." It is a name linked with strength and protection.

3. Amari: A Swahili name that means "strength and builder." It is a name connected with strength and willpower.

4. Andy is a Greek name that means "manly". It is a name linked with strength and masculinity.

5. Arden is an English name that means "eagle valley." It's a name connected with independence and strength.

6. Ariel is a Hebrew name that means "God's lion." It is a name linked with strength and force.

7. Ash: a name that means "ash tree" in English. It's a name linked to nature and the environment.

8. Aspen: a name that means "quaking tree" in English. It's a name linked to nature and the environment.

9. Aubrey: a French name that means "ruler of the elves." It's a name synonymous with wisdom and leadership.

10. August is a Latin name that means "great" or "magnificent". It is a name linked with power and strength.

11. Avery is an English name that means "ruler of the elves." It's a name synonymous with wisdom and leadership.

12. Bailey is an English name that means "bailiff" or "steward". It's a name that connotes responsibility and leadership.

13. Blair is a Scottish name that means "plain" or "field." It's a name linked to nature and the environment.

14. Blake is an English name that means "dark" or "black." It is a name linked with power and strength.

15. Cameron is a Scottish name that means "crooked nose." It is a name connected with fortitude and perseverance.

16. Casey is an Irish name that means "brave". It is a name that is connected with bravery and strength.

17. Charlie: an English name that means "free man" It's a name synonymous with liberty and independence.

18. Dakota is a Native American name that means "friends" or "allies." It is a name connected with harmony and tranquility.

19. Dallas is a Scottish name that means "meadow dwelling." It's a name linked to nature and the environment.

20. Dana is an Irish name that means "bold" or "wise". It is a name that is connected with knowledge and bravery.

21. Dylan is a Welsh name that means "son of the sea." It's a name linked to nature and the environment.

22. Eden is a Hebrew name that means "delight". It is a name connected with joy and happiness.

23. Elliot is a Scottish name that means "the Lord is my God." It is a name linked with power and strength.

24. Emerson is an English name that means "son of Emery". It is a name connected with fortitude and perseverance.

25. Finley is a Scottish name that means "fair-haired hero." It is a name linked with bravery and strength.

26. Frankie: an English name that means "free man" It's a name synonymous with liberty and independence.

27. Gray is an English name that means "gray-haired". It's a name synonymous with wisdom and expertise.

28. Hadley is an English name that means "heather meadow". It's a name linked to nature and the environment.

29. Harper is an English name that means "harp player." It's a name linked to music and creativity.

30. Hayden is an English name that means "heather-grown hill." It's a name linked to nature and the environment.

31. Hunter is an English name that means "one who hunts." It is a name connected with power and ability.

32. Indigo is a Greek name that means "Indian dye." It is a name connected with originality and innovation.

33. Jamie is a Scottish name that means "supplanter." It's a name that connotes strength and resolve.

34. Jordan is a Hebrew name that means "to flow down". It is a name connected

with fortitude and perseverance.

35. Jules is a French name that means "youthful." It is a name connected with vitality and energy.

36. Kai is a Hawaiian name that means "sea". It's a name linked to nature and the environment.

37. Kendall is an English name that means "Valley of the River Kent". It's a name linked to nature and the environment.

38. Kennedy: an Irish name that means "helmeted chief." It is a name linked with strength and leadership.

39. Lane: a name that means "narrow road" in English. It is a name connected with purpose and direction.

40. Logan is a Scottish name that means "little hollow." It's a name linked to nature and the environment.

41. London: is an English name that means "moon fortress." It is a name linked with power and strength.

42. Marley: an English name that means "pleasant wood." It's a name linked to nature and the environment.

43. Morgan is a Welsh name that means "sea-born." It's a name linked to nature and the environment.

44. Parker is an English name that means "keeper of the park." It's a name linked to nature and the environment.

45. Payton: an English name that means "warrior village." It is a name connected with fortitude and perseverance.

46. Phoenix is a Greek name that means "dark red." It is a name that is connected with power and rebirth.

47. Quinn is an Irish name that means "wise". It's a name that connotes knowledge and wisdom.

48. Reese is a Welsh name that means "enthusiasm." It is a name linked with vigor and zeal.

49. Riley is an Irish name that means "courageous". It is a name linked with bravery and strength.

50. River is an English name that means "flowing water." It's a name linked to nature and the environment.

51. Robin is an English name that means "bright fame." It's a name that connotes brilliance and creativity.

52. Rory is an Irish name that means "red king." It is a name linked with power and strength.

53. Rowan is a Gaelic name that means "little red one." It's a name linked to nature and the environment.

54. Ryan is an Irish name that means "little king." It is a name linked with power and authority.

55. Sage is a name that means "wise one" in English. It's a name that connotes knowledge and wisdom.

56. Sam is a Hebrew name that means "heard by God." It is a name connected with fortitude and perseverance.

57. Sawyer is an English name that means "woodcutter." It's a name linked to nature and the environment.

58 Scout is a name that means "to listen" in English. It is a name that connotes intelligence and awareness.

59. Skylar is a name that means "scholar" in English. It is a name that connotes intelligence and learning.

60. Sloane is an Irish name that means "warrior." It is a name linked with bravery and strength.

61. Spencer is an English name that means "steward". It's a name that connotes responsibility and leadership.

62. Sydney is an English name that means "wide island." It's a name linked to nature and the environment.

63. Taylor is an English name that means "tailor". It is a name connected with talent and innovation.

64. Teagan is a Welsh name that means "attractive". It's a name synonymous with beauty and charm.

65. Tegan is a Welsh name that means "fair". It is a name linked with grace and beauty.

66. Tyler is an English name that means "tile maker." It is a name connected with talent and innovation.

67. Wren is an English name that means "small bird." It's a name linked to nature and the environment.

68. Wyatt is an English name that means "brave in battle." It is a name linked with bravery and strength.

International Names: Europe

1. Adelaide: A Germanic name that means "of noble birth" or "of noble kind." Adelaide was the name of an Italian queen in the tenth century, and it is also the capital city of South Australia.

2. Adele: A Germanic name that means "noble" or "kind". Adele is a popular name that has been passed down through generations, with notable bearers including singer Adele.

3. Agnes: A Greek name that means "pure" or "chaste". Saint Agnes is a famous bearer of the name Agnes, which has been popular for centuries.

4. Alexandra: A Greek name that means "people's defender." Alexandra is a popular name that has been passed down through generations, with notable bearers including Queen Alexandra of England.

5. Alice: A Germanic name that means "noble" or "kind". Alice is a traditional name that has been used for centuries, and notable bearers include author Alice Walker.

6. Amelia: is a Germanic name that means "work." Amelia has been a popular name since the nineteenth century, with notable bearers including pilot Amelia Earhart.

7. Anastasia: is a Greek name that means "resurrection." Anastasia has been a popular name since the early twentieth century, with notable bearers including Grand Duchess Anastasia of Russia.

8. Andrea: A Greek name that means "manly" or "warrior". Andrea has been a popular unisex name since the mid-twentieth century, with notable bearers including actress Andrea Riseborough.

9. Anna: which means "grace" in Hebrew. Anna is a traditional name that has been used for centuries, and notable bearers include author Anna Karenina.

10. Aurora: is a Latin name that means "dawn". Aurora has been a popular name since the nineteenth century, with notable bearers including actress Aurora Perrineau.

11. Barbara: A Greek name that means "foreign" or "abnormal." Barbara is a popular name that has been passed down through generations, with notable bearers including singer Barbara Streisand.

12. Beatrice: is a Latin name that means "she who brings happiness." Beatrice is a popular name that has been passed down through generations, with notable bearers including author Beatrice Potter.

13. Bella: is an Italian name that means "beautiful". Bella is a popular name since the early twenty-first century, with notable bearers including actress Bella Thorne.

14. Bethany: A Hebrew name that means "house of figs." Bethany has been a popular name since the mid-twentieth century, with notable bearers including actress Bethany Joy Lenz.

15. Bianca: An Italian name that means "white." Bianca has been a popular name since the 16th century, and notable bearers include actress Bianca Lawson.

16. Blanca: is a Spanish name that means "white". Blanca has been a popular name since the nineteenth century, with notable bearers including actress Blanca Suarez.

17. Bridget: is an Irish name that means "exalted one". Bridget has been a popular name since the twentieth century, with notable bearers including actress Bridget Moynahan.

18. Brigitte: is a French name that means "exalted one". Brigitte has been a popular name since the mid-twentieth century, with notable bearers including actress Brigitte Bardot.

19. Bronwen: is a Welsh name that means "white breast". Bronwen has been a popular name since the twentieth century, with notable bearers including author Bronwen Wallace.

20. Bryony: is a Greek name that means "to sprout." Bryony has been a popular name since the twentieth century, with notable bearers including actress Bryony Hannah.

21. Camilla: Latin name meaning "young ceremonial attendant". Camilla is a popular name dating back to the 18th century, with notable bearers including Duchess Camilla of Cornwall.

22. Catherine: is a Greek name that means "pure". Catherine is a traditional name that has been used for centuries, and notable bearers include Catherine the Great of Russia.

23. Cecilia: is a Latin name that means "blind". Cecilia has been a popular name since the nineteenth century, with notable bearers including singer Cecilia Bartoli.

24. Celine: is a French name that means "heavenly". Celine has been a popular name since the twentieth century, with notable bearers including singer Celine Dion.

25. Charlotte: is a French name that means "free man." Charlotte is a popular name dating back to the 18th century, with notable bearers including Princess Charlotte of Cambridge.

26. Chloe: is a Greek name that means "blooming". Chloe has been a popular name since the late twentieth century, with notable bearers including actress Chloe Sevigny.

27. Clara: is a Latin name that means "clear" or "bright". Clara is a popular name

that has been passed down through generations, with notable bearers including composer Clara Schumann.

28. Constance: is a Latin name that means "constant" or "steadfast". Constance has been a popular name since the nineteenth century, with notable bearers including actress Constance Wu.

29. Cordelia: is a Celtic name that means "heart" or "daughter of the sea." Cordelia has been a popular name since the nineteenth century, with notable bearers including actress Cordelia Bugeja.

30. Cosima: An Italian name that means "order" or "beauty". Cosima has been a popular name since the late 1800s, with notable bearers including composer Cosima Wagner.

31. Daisy: is a name that means "day's eye" in English. Daisy has been a popular name since the late 1800s, with notable bearers including actress Daisy Ridley.

32. Danielle: is a Hebrew name that means "God is my judge." Danielle has been a popular name since the mid-twentieth century, with notable bearers including actress Danielle Panabaker.

33. Daphne: is a Greek name that means "laurel". Daphne has been a popular name since the nineteenth century, with notable bearers including author Daphne du Maurier.

34. Deborah: is a Hebrew name that means "bee". Deborah has been a popular name since the mid-twentieth century, with notable bearers including actress Deborah Ann Woll.

35. Delilah: is a Hebrew name that means "delicate". Delilah has been a popular name since the late twentieth century, with notable bearers including singer Delilah Montagu.

36. Delphine: is a French name that means "dolphin". Delphine has been a popular name since the mid-twentieth century, with notable bearers including actress Delphine Seyrig.

37. Denise: is a French name that means "follower of Dionysus." Denise has been a popular name since the mid-twentieth century, with notable bearers including actress Denise Richards.

38. Diana: is a Latin name that means "divine". Diana is a popular name that has been passed down through generations, with notable bearers including Princess Diana of Wales.

39. Dominique: is a French name that means "belonging to the Lord." Dominique has been a popular name since the mid-twentieth century, with notable bearers including singer Dominique A.

40. Dora: is a Greek name that means "gift". Dora has been a popular name since the nineteenth century, with notable bearers including author Dora Carrington.

41. Eleanor: is a Greek name that means "bright one" or "shining one." It was derived from the name Aliénor, which Eleanor of Aquitaine brought to England.

42. Elena: is a Greek name that means "bright one" or "shining one." It is the Spanish and Italian spelling of Helen.

43. Elisa: This is a Spanish, Italian, and Portuguese spelling of Elizabeth. It means "sworn to God."

44. Elizabeth: The Hebrew name Elizabeth means "God is my oath." Many queens and princesses have used this name throughout history.

45. Emily: This is a Latin name that means "rival". It is a well-known name that has been in use since the nineteenth century.

46. Emma: is a Germanic name that means "complete" or "universal." Since the nineteenth century, it has been a popular name in England.

47. Erica: is a Norse name that means "ruler of all". It's a name that dates back to the Middle Ages.

48. Esther: is a Hebrew name that means "star". It is the name of a biblical figure who rose to become Queen of Persia.

49. Eva: is a Hebrew name that means "life." It is the biblical name for the first woman.

50. Eveline: A French variant of the name Evelyn that means "hazelnut."

51. Faye: An Old English name meaning "fairy" or "elf." Poet Thomas Hood popularized it in the nineteenth century.

52. Felicity: is a Latin name that means "happiness" or "luck." During the Puritan era, it was a popular name.

53. Fiona: is a Scottish name that means "fair" or "white". The character Fiona in the novel "The Lion, the Witch, and the Wardrobe" popularized it in the twentieth century.

54. Fleur: is a French name that means "flower." Fleur Delacour, a character in the Harry Potter series, popularized it.

55. Flora: This is a Latin name that means "flower". It is the name of the Roman goddess of spring and flowers.

56. Florence: is a Latin name that means "thriving" or "prosperous." During the Renaissance, the Italian city of Florence popularized it.

57. Frances: is a Latin name that means "from France." It was a popular name in the

nineteenth century.

58. Francesca: is an Italian variation of the name Frances. It means "from France".

59. Frederica: A Germanic name meaning "peaceful ruler." The Prussian queen Frederica Louisa popularized it in the 18th century.

60. Frieda: is a Germanic name that means "peace". Frieda Lawrence popularized it in the twentieth century.

61. Gabriella: is a Hebrew name that means "God is my strength." It is Gabriel's feminine form.

62. Gemma: This is a Latin name that means "gem" or "precious stone". Gemma Hardy, a British writer, popularized it in the nineteenth century.

63. Genevieve: is a French name that means "white wave." Saint Genevieve, the patron saint of Paris, popularized it in the Middle Ages.

64. Georgia: A Greek name that means "farmer" or "earth-worker." It is the name of a state in the United States, and it was popularized by the British monarch George III.

65. Giselle: is a Germanic name that means "pledge." The ballet "Giselle" popularized it in the nineteenth century.

66. Gloria: is a Latin name that means "glory". The actress Gloria Swanson popularized it in the twentieth century.

67. Grace: is a Latin name that means "grace" or "favor". The Puritans popularized it in the 17th century.

68. Greta: is a Germanic name that means "pearl". Greta Garbo made it popular in the twentieth century.

69. Gwendolyn: is a Welsh name that means "white ring." Gwendolyn Brooks popularized it in the twentieth century.

70. Hannah: is a Hebrew name that means "grace" or "favor". It is the name of a biblical figure.

71. Harriet: is a French name that means "ruler of the house." Harriet Tubman, an abolitionist, popularized it in the nineteenth century.

72. Hazel: An Old English name meaning "hazel tree." The character Hazel from the comic strip "Little Orphan Annie" popularized it in the early twentieth century.

72. Heidi: is a Swiss name that means "of noble birth." The novel "Heidi" popularized it in the nineteenth century.

74. Helen: is a Greek name that means "bright one" or "shining one." It is the name of a character in Greek mythology, and the British Queen Victoria popularized it in

Greek mythology, and the British Queen Victoria popularized it in the nineteenth century.

75. Henrietta: is a French name that means "ruler of the house." The British queen Henrietta Maria popularized it in the 18th century.

76. Hermione: is a Greek name that means "messenger" or "earthly". It is the name of a character from Greek mythology, and it was popularized in the twentieth century by Hermione in the Harry Potter series.

77. Holly: is an Old English name that means "holly tree." It is frequently associated with Christmas and was made popular in the twentieth century by actress Holly Hunter.

78. Honor: This is a Latin name that means "honor" or "dignity". The Puritans popularized it in the 17th century.

79. Hope: is a name that means "hope" in English. The Puritans popularized it in the 17th century.

80. Ida: This is an Old Germanic name that means "hard worker." The novel "Ida May" popularized it in the nineteenth century.

81. Ilaria: An Italian name that means "joyful" or "happy." The actress Ilaria Occhini popularized it in the twentieth century.

82. Imogen: is a Celtic name that means "maiden". The poet William Shakespeare popularized it in the 17th century.

83. Indira: is a Sanskrit name that means "beauty" or "splendor". Indira Gandhi, India's first female prime minister, bore this name.

84. Ingrid: is a Norse name that means "beautiful" or "beloved". The actress Ingrid Bergman popularized it in the twentieth century.

Irene is a Greek name that means "peace". Irene Nemirovsky, a British writer, popularized it in the nineteenth century.

86. Isabella: This is an Italian variant of Isabel that means "God is my oath." The character Isabella Thorpe in the novel "Northanger Abbey" popularized it in the nineteenth century.

87. Isla: This Scottish name means "island." The actress Isla Fisher popularized it in the twenty-first century.

88. Ivana: is a Slavic name that means "God is gracious." It was popularized in the twentieth century by businesswoman Ivana Trump.

89. Ivy: This is an Old English name that means "ivy plant." The character Ivy from the novel "East Lynne" popularized it in the nineteenth century.

90. Jacqueline: This is a French name that means "supplanter." It was popularized in the twentieth century by first lady Jacqueline Kennedy.

91. Jade: This is a Spanish name that means "sidetone." Jade Jagger, an actress, popularized it in the twentieth century.

92. Jane: This is an English name that means "God is gracious." Jane Austen popularized it in the 19th century.

93. Jessica: is a Hebrew name that means "God beholds." The character Jessica in the play "The Merchant of Venice" popularized it in the twentieth century.

94. Joanna: This is a Hebrew name that means "God is gracious". The character Joanna from the television series "Dallas" popularized it in the twentieth century.

95. Jocelyn: This is an Old Germanic name that means "Gaut's tribe member." Jocelyn Brando popularized it in the twentieth century.

96. Josephine: This is a French feminine version of Joseph that means "God will add". The French empress Josephine popularized it in the nineteenth century.

97. Julia: is a Latin name that means "youthful" or "downy". The character Julia in the novel "Uncle Tom's Cabin" popularized it in the nineteenth century.

98. Juliet: A French diminutive of Julia that means "youthful."

99. Juniper: is a Latin word that means "youth-producing." It refers to a type of evergreen shrub or tiny tree.

100. Karolina: A Slavic name meaning "free man." It is the female version of the name Karl.

101. Kate: Kate is an English name that is a shortened version of Katherine. It translates as "pure" or "clear".

102. Katerina: This is a Greek variant of Katherine that means "pure."

103. Katherine: is a Greek name that means "pure". It has a long history of popularity, with noteworthy bearers including Catherine the Great and Kate Middleton.

104. Keira: is an Irish name that means "dark-haired". Keira Knightley popularized it in the twenty-first century.

105. Kimberly: This is an English name that means "from the royal forest's wood." It gained popularity in the twentieth century.

106. Kira: This Russian name means "throne." The actress Kira Ivanova popularized it in the twentieth century.

107. Kirsten: This is a Scandinavian name that means "Christ-follower." The actress Kirsten Dunst popularized it in the twentieth century.

108. Klara: A German name that means "clear" or "bright". Saint Clare of Assisi popularized it in the 13th century.

109. Kristina: This is a spelling variation of Christina, which means "Christ-follower." It gained popularity in the twentieth century.

110. Laura: is a Latin name that means "laurel" in English. Laura Ingalls Wilder popularized it in the nineteenth century.

111. Lea: This is a Hebrew name that means "weary". The actress Lea Thompson popularized it in the twentieth century.

112. Leah: A Hebrew name that means "tired." It is the name of a biblical figure.

113. Lena: A Greek name that means "light" The actress Lena Horne popularized it in the twentieth century.

114. Lillian: is an English name that means "lily". It gained popularity in the nineteenth century.

115. Lily: An English name that means "lily". It gained popularity in the nineteenth century.

116. Lorelei: is a German name that means "alluring enchantress". It is the name of a Rhine River rock associated with a legendary siren.

117. Louise: is a French name that means "renowned warrior." Queen Victoria of the United Kingdom popularized it in the nineteenth century.

118. Lucy: This is an English name that means "light". It gained popularity in the nineteenth century.

119. Lydia: is a Greek name that means "from Lydia". Lydia Bennet's character in the novel "Pride and Prejudice" popularized it in the nineteenth century.

120. Madeleine: is a French name that means "of Magdala." It gained popularity in the nineteenth century.

121. Margaret: is an English name that means "pearl". It has a long history of popularity, with noteworthy bearers including Margaret Thatcher and Margaret Atwood.

122. Maria: is a Latin name that means "sea of bitterness" or "rebelliousness." In the Bible, it is the name of Jesus' mother.

123. Matilda: is a Germanic name that means "mighty in battle." Empress Matilda popularized it in the 11th century.

124. Megan: A Welsh name that means "pearl" It gained popularity in the twentieth century.

125. Melanie: is a Greek name that means "dark" or "black". It gained popularity in

the twentieth century.

126. Mia: This is a Scandinavian name that means "mine" or "beloved". Mia Wasikowska popularized it in the twenty-first century.

127. Mila is a Slavic name that means "gracious" or "dear". Mila Kunis popularized it in the twenty-first century.

128. Miranda: is a Latin name that means "adorable" or "wonderful." It gained popularity in the twentieth century.

129. Molly: is an English name that means "bitter". It gained popularity in the twentieth century.

130. Nadine: is a French name that means "hope". It gained popularity in the twentieth century.

131. Naomi: is a Hebrew name that means "pleasantness." It is the name of a biblical figure.

132. Natalia: A Latin name that means "born on Christmas day." It gained popularity in the twentieth century.

133. Natalie: is a spelling variation of Natalia, which means "born on Christmas day." It gained popularity in the twentieth century.

134. Natasha: A Russian diminutive of Natalia that means "born on Christmas day." It gained popularity in the twentieth century.

135. Niamh: This is an Irish name that means "bright" or "radiant". It is a mythological princess's name.

136. Nicole: is a French name that means "victorious people." It gained popularity in the twentieth century.

137. Nina: is a Russian name that means "grace". It gained popularity in the twentieth century.

138. Noelle: A French name that means "Christmas" It gained popularity in the twentieth century.

139. Nora: is an Irish name that means "honor" or "dignity." It gained popularity in the nineteenth century.

140. Octavia: is a Latin name that means "eighth". It gained popularity in the nineteenth century.

141. Odette: is a French name that means "rich." The name comes from a character in the ballet "Swan Lake."

142. Olesia: This Slavic name means "protector." It gained popularity in the twentieth century.

143. Olivia: is a Latin name that means "olive tree". It has a long history of popularity, with noteworthy bearers including Olivia de Havilland and Olivia Newton-John.

144. Olympia: is a Greek name that means "from Mount Olympus." It gained popularity in the nineteenth century.

145. Ona: is a Lithuanian name that means "grace". It gained popularity in the twentieth century.

146. Oona: An Irish name that means "one" It gained popularity in the twentieth century.

147. Ophelia: is a Greek name that means "help" or "aid". It is a character name in Shakespeare's play "Hamlet."

148. Oriana: is a Latin name that means "golden". It gained popularity in the nineteenth century.

149. Orla: is an Irish name that means "golden princess." It gained popularity in the twentieth century.

150. Paige: is an English name that means "servant" or "page". It gained popularity in the twentieth century.

151. Patricia: is a Latin name that means "noble". It gained popularity in the twentieth century.

152. Pauline: is a Latin name that means "small". It gained popularity in the nineteenth century.

153. Penelope: A Greek name meaning "weaver." It is the name of a Greek mythological character.

154. Petra: Petra is a Greek name that means "rock." It gained popularity in the twentieth century.

155. Phoebe: A Greek name that means "bright" or "shining". It gained popularity in the twentieth century.

156. Polly: is an English name that means "small" or "humble". It gained popularity in the nineteenth century.

157. Portia: This is a Latin name that means "pig". It is a character name in Shakespeare's play "The Merchant of Venice."

158. Primrose: This is an English term for the flower of the same name. It gained popularity in the nineteenth century.

159. Priscilla: is a Latin name that means "ancient" or "venerable". It gained popularity in the twentieth century.

160. Qiana: This is a contemporary name from the 1970s. Its origin and significance are unknown.

161. Queenie: A nickname meaning "queen-like." It gained popularity in the nineteenth century.

162. Quenby: is an English name that means "woman's estate." It gained popularity in the nineteenth century.

163. Querida: A Spanish name that means "loved." It gained popularity in the twentieth century.

165. Quetzal: This is a Nahuatl word for the bird of the same name. It gained popularity in the twentieth century.

166. Quiana: This is a contemporary name from the 1970s. Its origin and significance are unknown.

167. Quilla: This is a Quechua name that means "moon." It gained popularity in the twentieth century.

167. Quinlan: is an Irish name that means "fit-shaped." It gained popularity in the twentieth century.

168. Quinn: is an Irish name that means "descendant of Conn." It gained popularity in the twentieth century.

169. Rachel: is a Hebrew name that means "ewe". It is the name of a biblical figure.

170. Ramona: is a Spanish name that means "wise protector." It gained popularity in the nineteenth century.

171. Rebecca: is a Hebrew name that means "to bind" or "to tie". It is the name of a biblical figure.

172. Regina: is a Latin name that means "queen". It gained popularity in the nineteenth century.

173. Renata: is a Latin name that means "reborn". It gained popularity in the twentieth century.

174. Rosalie: is a French name that means "rose". It gained popularity in the nineteenth century.

175. Rosalind: is a Latin name that means "pretty rose". It gained popularity in the nineteenth century.

176. Rose: This is an English term that relates to the same-named flower. It gained popularity in the nineteenth century.

177. Ruby: This is an English name for the gemstone of the same name. It gained popularity in the nineteenth century.

178. Ruthv is a Hebrew name that means "companion" or "friend". It is the name of a biblical figure.

179. Sabrina: is a Welsh name that means "legendary princess." It gained popularity in the twentieth century.

180. Sarah: is a Hebrew name that means "princess." It is the name of a biblical figure.

181. Selena: This is a Latin name that means "moon". It gained popularity in the twentieth century.

182. Simone: This is a French name that means "heard". It gained popularity in the twentieth century.

184. Sofia: is a Greek name that means "wisdom." It gained popularity in the twentieth century.

184. Sophia: This Greek name signifies "wisdom." It gained popularity in the nineteenth century.

185. Stella: is a Latin name that means "star". It gained popularity in the nineteenth century.

186. Stephanie: is a Greek name that means "crown" or "garland". It gained popularity in the twentieth century.

187. Susan: is a Hebrew name that means "lily". It gained popularity in the twentieth century.

188. Sylvia: A Latin name that means "from the forest." It gained popularity in the nineteenth century.

189. Tabitha: This is a Hebrew name that means "gazelle". It is the name of a biblical figure.

190. Talia: is a Hebrew name that means "dew from God." It gained popularity in the twentieth century.

191. Tamsin: A Cornish name that means "twin". It gained popularity in the twentieth century.

192. Tatiana: is a Russian name that means "fairy queen." It gained popularity in the twentieth century.

193. Teresa: is a Spanish name that translates as "harvester." It gained popularity in the twentieth century.

194. Tessa: is a shortened version of the name Theresa. It gained popularity in the twentieth century.

195. Thalia: A Greek name meaning "to flourish." It gained popularity in the

twentieth century.

196. Thea: A Greek name that means "goddess." It gained popularity in the twentieth century.

197. Tiffany: This is an English name that means "manifestation of God". It gained popularity in the twentieth century.

198. Trista: This is a Latin name that means "sad" or "sorrowful". It gained popularity in the twentieth century.

199. Uliana: This is a Russian name that means "youthful". It gained popularity in the twentieth century.

200. Ulla: is a Scandinavian name that means "willpower." It gained popularity in the twentieth century.

201. Ulrika: is a Scandinavian name that means "wolf power." It gained popularity in the twentieth century.

202. Ulyana: This Russian name means "youthful." It gained popularity in the twentieth century.

203. Umi: This Japanese name means "ocean." It gained popularity in the twentieth century.

204. Una: is an Irish name that means "one" or "unity." It gained popularity in the nineteenth century.

205. Urielle: is a Hebrew name that means "God is my light." It gained popularity in the twentieth century.

206. Ursula: Ursula is a Latin name that means "little bear." It gained popularity in the nineteenth century.

207. Ute: This is a German name that means "prosperous". It gained popularity in the twentieth century.

208. Valentina: is a Latin name that means "strong" or "healthy". It gained popularity in the twentieth century.

209. Valeria: is a Latin name that means "strong" or "healthy". It gained popularity in the nineteenth century.

210. Valerie: is a Latin name that means "strong" or "healthy". It gained popularity in the twentieth century.

211. Vanessa: This is a made-up name popularized by author Jonathan Swift. Its meaning is obscure.

212. Vera: is a Russian name that means "faith". It gained popularity in the twentieth century.

213. Vicky: is a shortened version of the name Victoria. It gained popularity in the twentieth century.

214. Victoria: is a Latin name that means "victory." It gained popularity in the nineteenth century.

215. Vida: is a Spanish name that means "life." It gained popularity in the twentieth century.

216. Violet: This is an English term for the flower of the same name. It gained popularity in the nineteenth century.

217. Vivienne: is a French name that means "alive" or "lively". It gained popularity in the twentieth century.

218. Wendy: is a made-up name that originally appeared in J.M. Barrie's "Peter Pan." Its meaning is obscure.

219. Whitney: is a name that means "white island" in English. It gained popularity in the twentieth century.

220. Wilhelmina: is a German name that means "will" or "helmet". It gained popularity in the nineteenth century.

221. Winifred: is a Welsh name that means "blessed peacemaker." It gained popularity in the nineteenth century.

222. Wren: This is an English name for a bird of the same name. It gained popularity in the twentieth century.

223. Xanthe: is A Greek name that means "yellow."

International Names: Celtic

1. Adair: Adair is a Scottish surname that means "oak tree ford" or "from the oak tree ford."

2. Aderyn: a Welsh name that means "bird"

3. Aeron: a Welsh name that means "berry" or "fruit".

4. Ailsa: is a Scottish name that means "elf victory" or "Alfs' island."

5. Aine: An Irish name that means "radiance" or "splendor".

6. Aisling: is an Irish name that means "dream" or "vision".

7. Alana: is a Hawaiian name that means "awakening" or "precious".

8. Alanna: is a variation of Alana with the same meaning.

9. Anya: is a Russian name that means "grace" or "favor".

10. Aoife: is an Irish name that means "beautiful" or "radiant".

11. Arwen: a Welsh name meaning "noble maiden" or "muse."

12. Ashling: an Irish name that means "dream" or "vision".

13. Bláthnaid: an Irish name meaning "little flower."

14. Branna: an Irish name that means "raven"

15. Branwen: a Welsh name meaning "beautiful raven."

16. Bree: is an Irish name that means "exalted" or "noble".

17. Bria: is a variation of Brianna with the same connotation of "noble" or "strong."

18. Brigid: is an Irish name that means "exalted one" or "strength".

19. Caitlin: an Irish name that means "pure" or "chaste".

20. Caoimhe: is an Irish name that means "gentle" or "beautiful".

21. Cara: is an Italian name that means "beloved" or "dear".

22. Carys: is a Welsh name that means "love" or "beloved".

23. Celyn: a Welsh name that means "holly"

24. Ceridwen: is a Welsh name that means "beautiful as a poem" or "fair and blessed".

25. Cerys: is a Welsh name that means "love" or "beloved".

26. Ciara: is an Irish name that means "dark-haired" or "black".

27. Cierra: is a variation of Sierra and has the same meaning as Sierra, which is "mountain."

28. Cliona: is an Irish name that means "shapely" or "beautiful".

29. Colleen: is an Irish name that means "girl" or "young woman".

30. Deirdre: an Irish name that means "sorrowful" or "broken-hearted".

31. Eibhlin: is an Irish name that means "pleasant" or "radiant".

32. Eileen: is an Irish name that means "shining one."

33. Eilidh: a Scottish name, that means "sun" or "radiant one."

34. Eilwen: is a Welsh name that means "fair brow" or "white brow."

35. Eira: is a Welsh name that means "snow" or "snowy".

36. Elowen: a Cornish name that means "elm tree"

37. Elspeth: a Scottish name that means "pledged to God" and is a version of the name Elizabeth.

38. Enfys: a Welsh name that means "rainbow"

32. Enya: is an Irish name that means "small fire."

40. Erin: an Irish name that signifies "peace" or "Ireland"

41. Finola: an Irish name meaning "white shoulder."

42. Fiona: a Scottish name that means "fair" or "white".

43. Glynis: a Welsh name meaning "valley" or "one who lives in the valley."

44. Gráinne: is an Irish name that means "grace".

45. Gwen: a Welsh name that means "white" or "blessed"

46. Gwendolyn: a Welsh name that means "blessed ring" or "white ring."

47. Gwennan: a Welsh name that means "blessed"

48. Gwyneira: is a Welsh name that means "white snow".

49. Idony: an English name that means "rejuvenation" or "renewal".

50. Imogen: is a Celtic name that means "maiden" or "innocent".

51. Iona: a Scottish name that means "blessed"

52. Iseult: a Celtic name meaning "fair lady" or "fair one."

53. Isla: is a Scottish name that means "island" or "river".

54. Isolde: is a Celtic name that means "fair lady" or "ice ruler."

55. Keira: an Irish name, that means "dark-haired" or "little dark one."

56. Kenna: is a Scottish name that means "born of fire" or "fire-born".

57. Kiera: is a variation of Keira with the same meaning.

58. Laoise: an Irish name meaning "radiant girl."

59. Ladan: an Irish name meaning "grey lady."

60. Luned: a Welsh name, that means "servant of the holy one."

61. Maeve: This name derives from the Irish and means "intoxicating" or "she who intoxicates".

62. Mairead: is an Irish name that means "pearl".

63. Mairin: is an Irish name that means "bitter" or "rebellious".

64. Méabh: which is of Irish origin, means "intoxicating" or "she who intoxicates."

65. Mererid: a Welsh name that means "pearl," is number 65.

66. Moira: This Irish name has connotations of bitterness or rebelliousness.

67. Morwen: is a Welsh name that means "maiden".

68. Nessa: is an Irish name that means "ambitious" or "not gentle".

69. Niamh: is an Irish name that means "bright" or "radiant".

70. Nola: an Irish name, has the meanings "famous" or "fair".

71. Olwen: a Welsh name that means "white footprint,"

72. Oona: an Irish name, that means "one" or "unity" in English.

73. Orla: an Irish name that means "golden princess"

74. Orlaghv an Irish name, means "golden lady" in English.

75. Rhian: a Welsh name that denotes "maiden" or "queen,"

76. Rhiannon: a Welsh name that means "great queen" or "divine queen,"

77. Rhona: is a Scottish name that means "rough island".

78. Róisn: is an Irish name that means "little rose".

79. Saoirse: is an Irish name that signifies "freedom".

80. Seren: which means "star" in Welsh.

81. Shannon: is an Irish name that means "wise river".

82. Sian: is a Welsh name meaning "God is gracious."

83. Sine: is a Scottish name that means "God is gracious".

84. Sinead: a name from Ireland that means "God is gracious."

85. Siobhan: is an Irish name that means "God is gracious".

86. Sofra: is an Irish name that means "changeling" or "little sprite".

87. Sorcha: is an Irish name that means "bright" or "radiant".

88. Taliesin: is a Welsh name that means "shining brow".

89. Tamsin: is a Cornish name meaning "twin".

90. Tara: which is of Irish origin, means "hill" or "tower."

91. Teagan: Teagan is a Welsh name that means "beautiful" or "attractive".

92. Tegan: a Welsh name that means "fair" or "beautiful,"

93. Teleri: is a Welsh name that means "shining brow".

94. Treasa: means "strong" or "courageous" in Irish.

95. Una: This Irish name denotes unity or oneness.

International Names: African

1. Aaliyah: This Arabic name means "high, exalted, sublime." It has grown in popularity in recent years, especially in the United States.

2. Abena: a name from Ghana that meaning "born on Tuesday."

3. Ada: a Germanic name meaning "noble, nobility."

4. Adama: a Hebrew name meaning "earth."

5. Adanna, an Igbo name, means "father's daughter."

6. Adenike: a Yoruba name meaning "the crown has come."

7. Adeola: This Yoruba name means "crown of wealth."

8. Adia is a Swahili name meaning "gift."

9. Adina, a Hebrew name, means "delicate, gentle."

10. Ajala: This Yoruba name means "wanderer."

11. Akua: Akan name meaning "born on Wednesday."

12. Alima: an Arabic name that meaning "wise, learned."

13. Amara: This Igbo name means "grace, mercy."

14. Amina: Amina is an Arabic name that means "trustworthy, faithful."

15. Asha: a Swahili name meaning "life."

16. Ayana is an Ethiopian name that translates as "beautiful flower."

17. Ayanna is a Swahili name that translates to "beautiful flower."

18. Ayodele is a Yoruba name that means "joy has come home."

19. Aysha is an Arabic name that means "living, life."

20. Binta is a Swahili word that means "with God."

21. Chidinma is an Igbo name that translates as "God is good."

22. Chika: an Igbo name that means "God is the greatest."

23. Chinyere: This Igbo name means "God gave."

24. Dalila is an Arabic name meaning "gentle, delicate."

25. Danica is a Slavic name meaning "morning star."

26. Ebony: is an English word for the ebony tree's dark, hardwood.

27. Efia, a Ghanaian name, means "born on Friday."

28. Eniola is a Yoruba name that means "person of wealth."

29. Esi: This Ghanaian name means "born on Sunday."

30. Fanta: This Swahili name means "beautiful."

31. Fatima: an Arabic name meaning "one who abstains."

32. Femi: This Yoruba name means "love me."

33. Halima: This Arabic name means "gentle, patient."

34. Ife is a Yoruba name meaning "love."

35. Ifeoma: This Igbo name means "good thing."

36. Imani: This Swahili name means "faith."

37. Imara: This Swahili name means "firm, strong."

38. Jamila: This Arabic name means "beautiful."

39. Jelani: a Swahili name meaning "mighty."

40. Kadija: The Arabic name Kadija means "early baby."

41. Kahina: an Arabic name meaning "priestess."

42. Kamaria: This Swahili name means "like the moon."

43. Kehinde, a Yoruba name, means "second-born twin."

44. Kemi: This Yoruba name means "mine."

45. Kenza: an Arabic name meaning "treasure."

46. Khadija: The Arabic name Khadija means "premature baby."

47. Kiana: a Hawaiian name meaning "divine."

48. Koko is a Japanese name that translates to "stork."

49. Kosi: an African name meaning "born on Sunday."

47. Kya, an African name, means "diamond in the sky."

51. Laila: This Arabic name means "night."

52. Lamia: an Arabic name meaning "shining."

53. Latifah: an Arabic name that means "kind, gentle."

54. Leila is an Arabic name meaning "night."

55. Leyla is an Arabic name meaning "night."

56. Liya: This Amharic name means "my God."

57. Malaika is a Swahili name meaning "angel."

58. Malika is an Arabic name meaning "queen."

59. Mariama: A Swahili name that meaning "God's gift."

60. Mazi: an Igbo name meaning "first daughter."

61. Mira: a Sanskrit name meaning "ocean, sea."

62. Mona is an Arabic name that means "wishes, desires."

63. Nabila: This Arabic name means "noble, eminent."

64. Nadia: This Arabic name signifies "hope."

65. Nada: This Arabic name means "hope."

65. Nala: This Swahili name means "successful."

66. Ngozi: This Igbo name means "blessing."

67. Nia: This Swahili name signifies "purpose."

68. Nkechi, an Igbo name, means "what God has given."

69. Nyla: This Arabic name means "winner."

70. Nyota: a Swahili name meaning "star."

71. Ogechi: This Igbo name signifies "God's time."

72. Ola: a Yoruba name meaning "wealth."

73. Oluchi: This Igbo name signifies "God's work."

74. Oluwakemi: This Yoruba name means "God has cared for me."

75. Oluwaseyi: This Yoruba name means "God made this."

76. Onika is a Native American name meaning "warrior."

77. Onyeka, an Igbo name that means "who is greater than God?"

78. Osayi: a Benin name meaning "God's gift."

79. Rahma: This is an Arabic name that means "mercy."

80. Rania is an Arabic name that translates as "queen."

81. Safiya: an Arabic name meaning "pure."

82. Sanaa is a Swahili name that translates to "art."

83. Saniyah: is an Arabic name that means "brilliant."

84. Selam: This Amharic name signifies "peace."

85. Sika: This Akan name means "money."

86. Simba is a Swahili name that translates to "lion."

87. Sisi is a Swahili name meaning "born on Sunday."

88. Sumara is an Arabic name that translates to "night conversation."

89. Tahira, an Arabic name, means "pure, chaste."

90. Tariro: Tariro is a Shona name that means "hope."

91. Teni is a Yoruba name meaning "crown."

92. Uchenna: This Igbo name signifies "God's will."

93. Umi: a Swahili name that meaning "life."

94. Yetunde, a Yoruba name, means "mother has returned."

95. Zahra: This Arabic name means "flower."

96. Zainab: This Arabic name means "fragrant flower."

97. Zara is an Arabic name meaning "princess."

98. Zawadi: a Swahili name meaning "gift."

99. Zola: This Zulu name means "quiet."

International Names: Asian

1. Aiko: is a Japanese name that translates as "beloved child."

2. Akira: is a Japanese name that translates as "smart, quick-witted."

3. Amara: is a Japanese name that means "eternal."

4. Anika: a Japanese name meaning "graceful."

5. Asuka: a Japanese name meaning "tomorrow's fragrance."

6. Ayako: is a Japanese name that translates as "colorful child."

7. Ayame: a Japanese name meaning "iris."

8. Ayumi: is a Japanese name that means "walk with beauty."

9. Chika: is a Japanese name that means "scattered flowers."

10. Chiyo: is a Japanese name that translates to "thousand generations."

11. Chiyoko: a Japanese name that translates as "child of a thousand generations."

12. Emi: is a Japanese name that translates to "beautiful blessing."

13. Erika: a Japanese name, that means "eternal ruler."

14 Eriko: Eriko is a Japanese name that means "child blessed with logic."

15. Fusako: is a Japanese name that translates as "helpful child."

16. Hana: is a Japanese name that translates to "flower."

17. Hanako: is a Japanese name that translates as "flower child."

18. Haruka: a Japanese name that means "distant."

19. Harumi: is a Japanese name that translates to "spring beauty."

20. Himari: is a Japanese name that translates to "good hollyhock."

21. Hiroko: is a Japanese name that translates as "abundant child."

22. Hitomi: is a Japanese name that means "pupil of the eye."

23. Honoka: is a Japanese name that translates to "harmony flower."

24. Hotaru: is a Japanese name that translates to "firefly."

25. Ichika: is a Japanese name that means "one thousand flowers."

26. Inari: is a Japanese name that translates as "successful."

27. Itsuk: is a Japanese name that translates as "timber tree."

28. Izumi: a Japanese name meaning "fountain."

29. Junko: is a Japanese name that translates as "pure child."

30. Kaida: is a Japanese name that translates as "little dragon."

31. Kaori: is a Japanese name that translates to "fragrance."

32. Kasumi: is a Japanese name that means "mist" or "haze".

33. Kazuko: (Japanese for "harmonious child") is a girl's name.

34. Keiko: a Japanese name meaning "blessed child."

35. Kiara: is a multi-ethnic name that means "bright" or "clear" in Japanese.

36. Kimiko: is a Japanese name that means "unrivaled child."

37. Kiyoko: a Japanese name meaning "pure child"

38. Kiyomi: a Japanese name that means "pure beauty".

39. Kohana: a Japanese name that translates as "little flower."

40. Kumi: a Japanese name that means "beautiful" or "long-lasting beauty."

41. Kyoko: a Japanese name meaning "respectful child."

42. Mai: is a Japanese name that means "to dance."

43. Maiko: is a Japanese name that means "dance child."

44. Maki: is a Japanese name that translates to "true hope."

45. Makoto: a Japanese name meaning "sincerity."

46. Mana: a name with several origins, including Japanese, that means "love" or "affection".

47. Mariko: is a Japanese name that means "true reason's child."

48. Megumi: a Japanese name that means "blessing".

49. Mei: is a Japanese name that means "beautiful" or "plum".

50. Michiko: is a Japanese name that translates to "beautiful wise child."

51. Miho: is a Japanese name that translates to "beautiful step."

53. Mikako: is a Japanese name that translates to "beautiful child."

54. Miki: is a Japanese name that translates to "beautiful princess."

55. Minako: a Japanese name that translates as "beautiful child."

56. Misaki: is a Japanese name that translates to "beautiful blossom."

57. Mizuki: a Japanese name that translates as "beautiful moon."

58. Momoko: is a Japanese name that translates as "peach child."

59. Nagisa: a Japanese name that means "beach"

60. Nana: is a Japanese name with several meanings, including "seven" and "vegetables."

61. Nanami: a Japanese name meaning "seven seas."

62. Naoko: a Japanese name that means "truthful child."

63. Naomi: is a Hebrew name that means "pleasantness" or "beauty."

64. Natsu: a Japanese name that means "summer"

65. Natsuki: is a Japanese name that can mean either "summer hope" or "summer moon."

66. Natsuko: a Japanese name that means "summer child"

67. Natsumi: a Japanese name that means "beautiful summer"

68. Noriko: is a Japanese name that means "law-abiding child."

69. Rei: is a Japanese name that can mean "beautiful" or "zero".

70. Reiko: is a Japanese name that means "thankful child."

71. Ren: is a Japanese name that means "lotus" or "love".

72. Riko: is a Japanese name that translates as "jasmine child."

73. Rin: is a Japanese name that can indicate either "dignified" or "cold."

74. Rina: is a Japanese name that means "jasmine" or "village".

75. Risa: is a Japanese name that means "village sand."

76. Sachiko: is a Japanese name that means "child of joy."

77. Saki: a Japanese name that means "blossom" or "hope".

78. Sakura: a Japanese name that means "cherry blossom"

79. Satomi: is a Japanese name that translates as "wise beauty."

80. Sayuri: is a Japanese name that translates to "small lily."

81. Setsuko: is a Japanese name that means "faithful child."

82. Shiori: is a Japanese name that translates to "bookmark."

83. Shoko: a Japanese name that means "fragrant child"

84. Suzu: is a Japanese name that means "bell".

85. Suzuka: a Japanese name that means "bellflower"

86. Takara: is a Japanese name that means "treasure".

87. Tamiko: is a Japanese name that translates as "child of many beauties."

88. Tomico: is a Japanese name that means "rich child."

89. Toshiko: is a Japanese name that means "wise child."

90. Tsuki: is a Japanese name that means "moon".

91. Umi: is a Japanese name that means "sea".

92. Yoko: is a Japanese name that means "child of the sun."

93. Yoriko: is a Japanese name that means "public child."

94. Yui: is a Japanese name that means "tie" or "bind".

95. Yuka: a Japanese name that means "fragrant" or "gentle".

96. Yukari: is a Japanese name that translates to "beautiful pear tree."

97. Yumi: is a Japanese name that means "archery bow".

98. Yumiko: is a Japanese name that means "beautiful child".

99. Yuri: a Japanese name that means "lily".

100. Yuriko: a Japanese name that means "lily child,"

International Names: Native American

1. Aiyana: is a Native American name that is commonly believed to mean "eternal blossom" or "forever flowering". However, the true meaning of the name is uncertain.

2. Alawa: is an Algonquin name that means "pea".

3. Amala: is a Sanskrit name that means "pure" or "unblemished".

4. Anaba: is an African name that means "she who returns from war".

5. Anevay: is a Native American name that means "superior" or "superiority".

6. Angeni: is a Cherokee name that means "spirit" or "angel".

7. Aponi: is a Native American name that means "butterfly".

8. Ayita: is a Cherokee name that means "first to dance".

9. Aylen: is a Mapuche name that means "clear" or "bright".

10. Catori: is a Native American name that means "spirit" or "ghost".

11. Chapa: is a Native American name that means "beaver".

12. Chenoa: is a Native American name that means "white dove".

13. Chilali: is a Native American name that means "snowbird".

14. Dyani: is a Native American name that means "deer".

15. Elu: is a Native American name that means "beautiful".

16. Etenia: is a Native American name that means "rich" or "wealthy".

17. Galilahi: is a Native American name that means "attractive" or "charming".

18. Halona: is a Native American name that means "happy fortune".

19. Halyn: is a Native American name that means "unique" or "one of a kind".

20. Hialeah: is a Native American name that means "pretty prairie".

21. Hok'ee: is a Native American name that means "abandoned" or "left behind".

22. Honiahaka: is a Native American name that means "little wolf".

23. Hehewuti: This is one of the popular Native American names and it means "warrior mother spirit".

24. Ichtaca: is an Aztec name that means "secret" or "mystery".

24. Ichtaca: is an Aztec name that means "secret" or "mystery".

25. Istas: is a Native American name that means "snow".

26. Kachina: is a Native American name that means "sacred dancer".

27. Koko: A Native American name that means "night".

28. Kaliska: is a Native American name that means "coyote chasing deer".

29. Kanti: is a Sanskrit name that means "beauty" or "radiance".

30. Kawena: is a Hawaiian name that means "glowing" or "shining".

31. Kaya: is a Native American name that means "my elder sister".

32. Kimimela: is a Native American name that means "butterfly".

33. Kinipela: is a Hawaiian name that means "wave".

34. Kiona: is a Native American name that means "brown hills".

35. Kishi: is a Japanese name that means "beach" or "shore".

36. Lenmana: is a Native American name that means "flute girl".

37. Leotie: is a Native American name that means "flower of the prairie".

38. Liluye: is a Native American name that means "wild dove".

39. Lulu: is a Swahili name that means "pearl".

40. Macha: is an Irish name that means "battle" or "warrior queen".

41. Maka: is a Native American name that means "earth".

42. Maska: is an Inuit name that means "strong".

43. Mika: is a Japanese name that means "beautiful fragrance".

44. Minowa: is a Native American name that means "rippling water".

45. Minta: is a Greek name that means "mint".

46. Moki: is a Hopi name that means "deer".

47. Nashoba: is a Native American name that means "wolf".

48. Natane: is a Native American name that means "daughter".

49. Neewa: is a Native American name that means "fourth-born".

50. Nita: is a Native American name that means "bear".

51. Nova: is a Latin name that means "new".

52. Ogin: is a Native American name that means "wild rose".

53. Ohanko: is a Native American name that means "resembling a star".

54. Onida: is a Native American name that means "the one searched for".

55. Osceola: is a Native American name that means "black drink crier".

56. Pakuna: is a Native American name that means "deer jumping downhill".

57. Patwin: is a Native American name that means "man".

58. Payat: is a Native American name that means "fire".

59. Peni: is a Hawaiian name that means "weaver".

60. Pocahontas: is a Native American name that means "playful one".

61. Qaletaqa: is a Hopi name that means "guardian of the people".

62. Quanah: is a Comanche name that means "fragrant".

63. Quetzal: is a Nahuatl name that means "precious feather".

64. Sacagawea: is a Native American name that means "bird woman".

65. Sahale: is a Native American name that means "above".

66. Salali: is a Cherokee name that means "squirrel".

67. Selu: is a Cherokee name that means "corn".

68. Sequoia: is a Cherokee name that means "sparrow".

69. Shilah: is a Native American name that means "brother".

70. Sitala: is a Hindi name that means "cool".

71. Talulah: is a Native American name that means "leaping water".

72. Tama: is a Japanese name that means "jewel".

73. Tansy: is an English name that means "herb".

74. Tatanka: is a Native American name that means "buffalo".

75. Tayanita: is a Native American name that means "young beaver".

76. Tekakwitha: is a Mohawk name that means "she who bumps into things".

77. Tsula: is a Cherokee name that means "fox".

78. Tunica: is a Native American name that means "little people".

79. Tuyet: is a Vietnamese name that means "snow".

80. Ulanni: is a Native American name that means "high".

81. Una: is a Latin name that means "one".

82. Usti: is a Native American name that means "woman".

83. Wakanda: is a Native American name that means "possesses magical powers".

84. Wamblee: is a Native American name that means "eagle".

85. Wayra: is a Native American name that means "wind".

86. Winema: is a Native American name that means "chief".

87. Winona: is a Native American name that means "first-born daughter".

88. Wren: is an English name that means "small bird".

89. Wyome: is a Native American name that means "large plain".

90. Yahoaholo: is a Native American name that means "one who yells.

91. Yoki: is a Native American name that means "rain".

92. Yonais: a Hebrew name that means "dove".

93. Zaltantana: is a Native American name that means "high mountain".

94. Zihna: is a Native American name that means "spins".

96. Zitkala: is a Native American name that means "bird".

Twin Names

1. Abigail and Amelia: Abigail means "my father's joy" and Amelia means "work".

2. Aria and Luna: Aria means "song" and Luna means "moon".

3. Aubrey and Audrey: Aubrey means "elf ruler" and Audrey means "noble strength".

4. Bella and Sophia: Bella means "beautiful" and Sophia means "wisdom".

5. Camila and Valentina: Camila means "free-born" and Valentina means "strong and healthy".

6. Charlotte and Caroline: Charlotte means "free man" and Caroline means "free woman".

7. Chloe and Zoey: Chloe means "blooming" and Zoey means "life".

8. Daisy and Lily: Daisy means "day's eye" and Lily means "pure".

9. Elena and Isabella: Elena means "bright, shining light" and Isabella means "God is my oath".

10. Elizabeth and Katherine: Elizabeth means "God's promise" and Katherine means "pure".

11. Emilia and Olivia: Emilia means "industrious" and Olivia means "olive tree".

12. Emma and Ella: Emma means "universal" and Ella means "light".

13. Faith and Grace: Faith means "belief" and Grace means "favor".

14. Gabriella and Isadora: Gabriella means "God is my strength" and Isadora means "gift of Isis".

15. Hailey and Hannah: Hailey means "hay meadow" and Hannah means "grace".

16. Harper and Piper: Harper means "harp player" and Piper means "flute player".

17. Hazel and Olive: Hazel means "hazelnut tree" and Olive means "olive tree".

18. Isla and Ivy: Isla means "island" and Ivy means "faithfulness".

19. Jade and Pearl: Jade means "stone of the side" and Pearl means "pearl".

20. Jasmine and Lily: Jasmine means "gift from God" and Lily means "pure".

21. Josephine and Madeline: Josephine means "God will increase" and Madeline means "high tower".

22. Julia and Juliana: Julia means "youthful" and Juliana means "youthful".

23. Kaitlyn and Kylie: Kaitlyn means "pure" and Kylie means "boomerang".

24. Kayla and Leah: Kayla means "keeper of the keys" and Leah means "weary".

25. Kennedy and Madison: Kennedy means "helmeted chief" and Madison means "son of Maud".

26. Lila and Layla: Lila means "night" and Layla means "night".

27. Lily and Rose: Lily means "pure" and Rose means "flower".

28. Lucy and Ruby: Lucy means "light" and Ruby means "red gemstone".

29. Mackenzie and McKenzie: Mackenzie means "son of the wise ruler" and McKenzie means "fair one".

30. Madelyn and Natalie: Madelyn means "high tower" and Natalie means "birthday of the Lord".

31. Mia and Sofia: Mia means "mine" and Sofia means "wisdom".

32. Mila and Lena: Mila means "gracious" and Lena means "bright".

33. Naomi and Noelle: Naomi means "pleasantness" and Noelle means "Christmas".

34. Nora and Sarah: Nora means "honor" and Sarah means "princess".

35. Paisley and Presley: Paisley means "church" and Presley means "priest's meadow".

36. Penelope and Persephone: Penelope means "weaver" and Persephone means "bringer of destruction".

37. Peyton and Taylor: Peyton means "fighting man's estate" and Taylor means "tailor".

38. Phoebe and Piper: Phoebe means "bright, shining" and Piper means "flute player".

39. Quinn and Reagan: Quinn means "wise" and Reagan means "little king".

40. Riley and Ryan: Riley means "valiant" and Ryan means "little king".

41. Rose and Violet: Rose means "flower" and Violet means "purple flower".

42. Ruby and Scarlett: Ruby means "red gemstone" and Scarlett means "scarlet cloth".

43. Samantha and Sabrina: Samantha means "listener" and Sabrina means "from the boundary river".

44. Savannah and Sierra: Savannah means "treeless plain" and Sierra means "mountain range".

45. Scarlett and Sienna: Scarlett means "scarlet cloth" and Sienna means "orange-red".

46. Serenity and Harmony: Serenity means "calmness" and Harmony means "agreement".

47. Skylar and Summer: Skylar means "scholar" and Summer means "warm season".

48. Sophia and Isabella: Sophia means "wisdom" and Isabella means "God is my oath".

49. Stella and Luna: Stella means "star" and Luna means "moon".

50. Sydney and Brooklyn: Sydney means "wide island" and Brooklyn means "water stream".

51. Tessa and Tess: Tessa means "harvester" and Tess means "to reap".

52. Trinity and Faith: Trinity means "threefold" and Faith means "belief".

53. Valentina and Victoria: Valentina means "strong and healthy" and Victoria means "victory".

54. Vanessa and Veronica: Vanessa means "butterfly" and Veronica means "true image".

55. Vivian and Violet: Vivian means "lively" and Violet means "purple flower".

56. Willow and Hazel: Willow means "willow tree" and Hazel means "hazelnut tree".

57. Winter and Autumn: Winter means "winter season" and Autumn means "fall season".

58. Zoe and Chloe: Zoe means "life" and Chloe means "blooming".

59. Zoey and Zara: Zoey means "life" and Zara means "princess".

60. Zuri and Zora: Zuri means "good" and Zora means "dawn".

10
TOP CHOICES NAME

Choice 1: _____

What characterizes this name?

_____

_____

Choice 2: _____

What characterizes this name?

_____

_____

Choice 3: _____

What characterizes this name?

_____

_____

Choice 4: _____

What characterizes this name?

_____

_____

Choice 5: _____

What characterizes this name?

_____

_____

10
TOP CHOICES NAME

Choice 6: _____

What characterizes this name?

_____

_____

Choice 7: _____

What characterizes this name?

_____

_____

Choice 8: _____

What characterizes this name?

_____

_____

Choice 9: _____

What characterizes this name?

_____

_____

Choice 10: _____

What characterizes this name?

_____

_____